ADVENTURE
AMERICA

PREVIOUS PAGE / A West Coast road trip leads to high adventures such as parachuting in California. ABOVE / Mountaineers climb Mount McKinley's Kahiltna Glacier in the Alaska Range, following the West Buttress Route on North America's highest mountain.

ADVENTURE
AMERICA

□ NATIONAL GEOGRAPHIC

WASHINGTON, D.C.

Giant red sandstone boulders, spalled from the cliffs above, stand sentinel over a pair of mountain bikers pedaling up Potash Road. Their destination: the rugged White Rim Trail in Canyonlands National Park, Utah.

Morning fog greets two paddlers exploring the Youghiogheny River during a five-day kayaking adventure in Maryland and Pennsylvania.

Wildflowers such as Indian paintbrush and columbine delight hikers as they embark on a three day llama-packing excursion in Idaho's and Wyoming's Teton Range.

Sun illuminates the cliffs at Pescadero State Beach, north of Santa Cruz, California, during a three-week motorcycling adventure up the West Coast of the United States.

Sunrise splashes a Green River campsite where cyclists on the White Rim Trail in Utah grabbed a well-earned pause from pedaling.

GREENLAND
(Denmark)

Labrador
Sea

Hudson
Bay

D A

eg

Lake
Superior

Ottawa ⊛

Lake
Ontario

Lake
Huron

L. Erie

Lake
Michigan

PENN.

New York

Pittsburgh

Philadelphia

T A T E S

Youghiogheny
River

MD.
⊛
Washington, DC

Ohio

ATLANTIC

OCEAN

Mississippi

0 _____ 500 miles

0 _____ 500 kilometers

A jet-powered Bell 206 helicopter carried
11 people to more than 10,000 feet during
a seven-day ski trip in central British
Columbia's snow-laden Purcell Mountains.

POWDER
PASSION

CHAPTER ONE

BY BERNADETTE McDONALD / PHOTOGRAPHS BY JOSÉ AZEL

WE FLEW through the clouds and mist, touching down on a gentle slope. "I can handle this," I assured myself. "I am going to ski like I normally do."

We ducked out of the helicopter, put on our skis, and pointed the tips downhill. Whirling snow, kicked up by the rotors, seemed so thick that it could suffocate us, yet through it I could still see an endless expanse of untracked snow.

Christjan Ladurner, our fit and compact guide, skied off smoothly—but a little slower than I would have expected for an expert. An Italian mountain man from Merano, Italy, he had been guiding for more than 15 years. He exuded a quiet confidence whether skiing, forecasting avalanche conditions, or analyzing terrain features for the best ski lines.

When he stopped 200 feet below and called for us to follow, he warned that the conditions were a little "crusty."

Crusty? It was horrendous! Because we were at a relatively low elevation, the snowpack had heated up during the previous day, become supersaturated, and had frozen overnight. It was now covered with a hard, breakable, icy top-layer. I tried a parallel turn, managed one, managed two more—then crashed through the crust. I mistakenly thought I would be able to stay on top because I was small and light.

LEFT / Skiers enjoy miles of untracked snow in the pristine wilderness of British Columbia's Bugaboo Mountains. ABOVE / Deep powder within a mature subalpine fir forest makes for ideal technical skiing conditions.

Extricating oneself from deep snow takes an enormous amount of energy. I hauled myself up once, then again, puffing heavily. This was clearly not working. Glancing up the slope I saw carnage: There were downed skiers everywhere. I made it to Christjan and mumbled something about the tricky conditions. He didn't respond but looked rather worried. How was he going to get this seemingly inept group down some of Canada's hardest terrain?

Thus began a new challenge, which would become my dream assignment—heli-skiing some of North America's most beautiful mountainous terrain in British Columbia's interior ranges. I'd been skiing for more than 20 years and was passionate about the sport. For ten of those years, while living in Jasper National Park in Alberta, Canada, I was on skis most winter days, and ever since I began my work in 1988 at The Banff Centre, I have managed to get out every weekend. I love all types of skiing; my skis allow me to move smoothly and efficiently on pristine snow through remote landscapes in winter, either alone or, most often, with a small group of friends.

In ski mountaineering, or ski touring as it's often called, one spends several hours slowly but steadily climbing mountains and hills with special skis and skins, which are put on the skis to help with traction. The reward is an incredible view and one exhilarating, well-earned run through untracked snow. This is what I was used to, and it was what I believed was the proper way to ski in the backcountry; but my perspective has changed. I've now had a taste of heli-skiing!

MY FIRST heli-skiing adventure began when I left my home in Banff, Alberta, and drove west along the Trans-Canada Highway through the Purcell and Selkirk Mountains, which are home to 14 heli-ski operations. At Revelstoke, British Columbia, I swung north from the highway and traveled ten miles up a wide, muddy logging road in the Goldstream Valley of the northern Selkirks. The only evidence of people was an abandoned copper mine compound, some logging high on a slope, and a level gravel parking lot that doubled as a heli-pad.

As the established rendezvous time neared, 40 fellow skiers drifted in from literally all four corners of the globe. We mingled at a makeshift wilderness cocktail party with coffee cups, sandwiches, introductions, and anticipation. Suddenly the air was filled with the *whop-whop* of a Bell 206 helicopter, and we piled in.

We ascended into the gray overcast of an early March storm and followed the serpentine course of the Goldstream River to an increasingly narrow valley. The clouds looked rather ominous. Moose were feeding on succulent willow branches that were beginning to emerge through the receding snowpack along the valley bottom. Within about ten minutes, we banked sharply left and caught sight of

a cozy lodge that would be our home for the next week. The lodge appeared high above the valley like a beacon made of stone, wood, and glass, signaling for us to land.

After settling in, we assembled in the common area for a safety lecture. We all came from different backgrounds, but I was clearly the neophyte among us. The outfitter, Canadian Mountain Holidays, had invited their best customers back for what they called Nostalgia Week. Several of the skiers said they had waited more than two years to be invited on this trip. Almost everyone had heli-skied before, some of them for as many as 30 years. Even so, our group of Canadian, Italian, French, and Austrian guides delivered a

lecture that was thorough: helicopter safety, how to avoid injury, what to do in case of an accident, how not to get lost, guide protocol—and probably the most important part—avalanche safety.

Even though everything is done to ensure the safety of heli-skiers, the reality was that we were in wild, steep, heavily snow-laden country, and this year in particular the avalanche hazard was high. Little snowfall and cold temperatures in early winter had created a loose and unstable base, providing a sliding surface

Certified mountain guide Dan Griffiths deals with storms, limited visibility, route finding, and avalanche forecasting every day as he leads clients through remote terrain in British Columbia.

for the later, heavier spring snow. The hazard was rated "extreme."

With transceivers, or beacons, dangling from our necks, we spent almost two hours reviewing what to do in case

Skiers enjoy not only challenging terrain, but also vistas of alpine peaks and snow-laden valleys in the Purcell Mountains.

of an avalanche and how to do speed searches for transceivers deeply buried in snowdrifts. This was vital because, in the event of an accident, each skier was expected to assume the role of rescuer. If anyone was buried in an avalanche, our abilities to locate and rescue were crucial to the victim's chances of survival. After a few minutes of being covered by a

AVALANCHE transceivers,

group dynamics, helicopter safety, guide protocol—my mind was beginning to overload. This was supposed to be fun.

That night I experienced a serious case of heli-stress. I hardly slept. I worried about the new skis I would be using. What about my skiing ability? Would I be the one whom everyone waited for as the helicopter hovered impatiently at the bottom of a run? Would I inadvertently kick a hole in the side of the helicopter?

Pale, hollow-eyed, and sleep deprived, I dragged myself to breakfast the next morning. As I looked out at the low cloud cover and snow squalls blowing through, I had a last-minute hope that skiing would be canceled for that day.

Wishful thinking. Everyone but me seemed excited. At breakfast I sat next to the founder of the company, Hans Gmoser, a slim, wiry mountain man with a spider's web of permanent laugh lines on his leathery face. He had emigrated to Canada from Austria in 1951 and soon established himself as a respected mountain guide and one of Canada's leading climbers. Hans is a quiet man with a crooked smile and twinkle in his eye. At 70 years old, his body has taken a lot of abuse from heavy packs, too many miles on the trails, millions of turns in varying snow conditions, and long, grueling expeditions. Yet the desire to explore his beloved mountains runs through him deep and strong.

snowslide, the probability of getting out alive drops exponentially. We were expected to organize ourselves, switch our transceivers from transmit to receive, spread out, head for the strongest audio signal, and systematically—via a grid pattern—hone in on the victim, without getting ourselves injured or killed. Serious stuff.

Spruce-hemlock forests thrive in more than 13 feet of snow for up to six months a year in the Bugaboo Mountains. Storms that roll in from the Pacific Coast frequently buffet this region of western Canada.

Before breakfast ended, Hans pressed on me a second helping of eggs Benedict and assured me that everything would be fine.

Actually I know Hans well, as he lives just a few miles down the road from my home in Banff, Alberta. I see him frequently on the cross-country ski trails. As a guide, he began the company that became Canadian Mountain Holidays in 1957—and some of his original clients were in the room that morning. Their fondness and respect for Hans was clear. He acted like he was in his own kitchen; this was the world he had created. As I munched my second croissant and chatted, I realized that many of the skiers came from traditional mountaineering backgrounds. This reassured me because I felt they would have an appreciation and respect for this wild mountain landscape. Although the group was high-powered, I noticed that if they had any attitudes, they left them at home. Italian and German businessmen, several American lawyers and pilots, and Canadians from across the country—it was an eclectic group.

I asked Hans why he chose the interior mountain ranges of British Columbia to set up his heli-skiing operation rather than the Rocky Mountains, where he actually lives. He explained how the snowpack in the Rockies is fundamentally different from that in British Columbia, where the storms roll in from the Pacific. By the time they get to the Rockies, most everything of value to a skier—snow—

has already dropped. The Selkirks, Monashees, Purcells, and Cariboo Mountains receive the bounty of those storms. Likewise, the temperatures are more moderate here, leading to a more stable snowpack. In fact, from all his traveling in the world's mountain ranges, Hans was convinced that the interior ranges of British Columbia offered the most consistent snow and the world's best skiing. That, combined with the wilderness of B.C., made it a natural choice. One of the greatest attractions of heli-skiing is the remoteness of the experience. The average area for any group of 44 skiers is 1,000 square miles. The heli-lodges are usually tucked high up the mountain, accessible only by helicopter or a four-wheel-drive vehicle.

DESPITE the relatively consistent snow conditions found in the interior ranges, there can be surprises. This winter, for instance, began slowly with almost no snow until January. During that drought, temperatures were lower than normal, often dropping below minus 13°F. These factors produced some unstable snow conditions, requiring guides with years of experience and in-depth knowledge of the terrain to ensure safety as well as good skiing for the guests. At pre-dawn meetings the guides analyzed every ski run, taking into account what direction they faced, how the previous night's temperatures and wind affected them,

and how much freezing and thawing they had undergone. With this information, the guides determined just which runs would be safe and would offer the lightest, driest, deepest snow. Once they made their decisions, their word was law—no disputing the guides.

This was vividly demonstrated by an incident in skier group number one. Before the clients descended their run as far as was navigable, the guide cut a traverse line in the snow with his skis, giving specific instructions not to go below it. The narrow, icy track wound around a rocky ridge to reach a small landing area for the helicopter. Below this traverse line were brush, trees, heavy wet snow, exposed rock, and water—not nice.

One of the most experienced skiers fell off the traverse line, and rather than climb back up to it, he tried to set a lower traverse line to join up with the others. His son followed him. Gravity pulled them lower and lower until they could no longer climb back up to the landing spot. The guide saw the rest of his group safely into the helicopter, then returned to investigate. Following their tracks, he quickly found them a hundred feet below the traverse line. Because of

Unusually warm spring temperatures weakened the complex structure of the snowpack, creating avalanche danger. This made a game of chess on the Bugaboo Lodge deck a much safer alternative to heli-skiing.

the thickly vegetated terrain, the helicopter was unable to rescue them. Now there was only one way out—down. It took them several hours of thrashing around through snow thick as mashed potatoes, complicated by exposed alder bushes, huge boulder fields, and babbling brooks—terrible skiing conditions! By the time they reached the lodge several hours later, they were exhausted.

Of course I knew nothing of this until much later, and meanwhile I was having my own adventures. Following our first, shall I say "challenging" descent, we reassembled, dusted ourselves off, and swallowed our humility pills. This is where the experience and training of our guide came through. Finding himself with a group of bedraggled, snow-covered, slightly discouraged skiers, Christjan suggested a different technique for the rest of the run, which, he assured us, would make it easier and safer to get down. He recommended that we follow his track; it would be a gently descending traverse line interspersed with a series of large S-curves. He would attempt to break through the crust at each curve so we wouldn't have to. He would execute the turns by utilizing an unglamorous technique called the snowplow. He advised us not to be too proud to snowplow, too.

I should have thought of it. I'm teased regularly by my ski-touring friends because I have the strongest snowplow in the valley. It's truly a very basic turn mastered by beginners, nothing sophisticated, but I do use it whenever the going

gets tough—and it always works. Obviously my ego had got in the way, as it never occurred to me to haul out my old snowplow technique in front of this worldly group of people.

As soon as I moved into this more stable position, everything improved. With my skis now pointed in a downhill "V," my weight was more evenly distributed and my movements were more fluid. I was able to stay almost completely on top of the crust. I descended the run comfortably, with energy left to admire the landscape into which we had been miraculously dropped. Snow-draped spruce and fir trees; softly undulating, sparkling white rolls under which huge rocks undoubtedly lurked; and ridge after ridge of cloud-wreathed wilderness filled my begoggled eyes.

I felt relieved to ski the run with only one spill. I knew from years of backcountry ventures that frequent falling is to be avoided. The energy consumption is staggering, and it's the quickest way to become severely tired and injure yourself. Stay upright at all costs.

Our helicopter pickup arrived and the cloud cover began to break up, so off we flew to a ridge about 3,000 feet higher. We dipped and turned, climbing steeply up valleys, only to drop abruptly over the narrow mountain passes. I found it difficult to stay oriented in relation to the lodge location, direction, and general whereabouts. I tried to see landmarks, register them, and lock them in my memory in case of an emergency. I knew

SNOW SAFETY

For heli-skiers, snow in the Purcell Mountains can be both fun and dangerous.

AVALANCHE HAZARD MANAGEMENT IN THE HELI-SKIING BUSINESS RELIES ON AN active, risk-avoidance methodology. Each morning, long before heli-skiing guests awaken, the mountain guides look over the latest computerized avalanche report originating from the Canadian Avalanche Association's office in Revelstoke, British Columbia. This report includes information about new snow, wind direction and speed, suspected weak layers in the snow, and any recent avalanche incidents.

The guides consult with each other extensively, then make a unanimous decision about what runs to ski that day. They also consult with other guides in neighboring areas to make a final, broader plan of action. They check a snow pit, a no-trespassing area where each day's snow can be measured, along with the accumulated snowpack and local wind and temperature information. (These snow pits may be dug by the guides at any time they feel the conditions are changing due to additional snow, winds, or unusual solar radiation.)

Every ski client is taught the basics of operating an avalanche transceiver, a device that will send a locator signal, if it is buried by snow to the other transceivers worn by those on the slopes. If a person, or a group, becomes buried in an avalanche, all other skiers must attempt immediate rescue. Every minute counts toward the victim's chances of survival. Meanwhile, neighboring heli-ski operations are notified, and any available guides and staff are immediately flown to the site to assist in a search.

All the guides are internationally qualified with years of training in avalanche safety. Avalanche forecasting is considered a convergence of science and art, best done by those with enormous experience in the mountains.

it wasn't my job, but my background as a ski mountaineer had me hardwired to know where I was at all times. It was simply impossible to keep my bearings, and it still bothers me how dependent I was on that pilot and his flying machine.

Upon landing, I realized there had been a miraculous improvement in the snow conditions. With excitement mounting, we strapped on our skis and tentatively moved off to the edge. We were perched on a high col between two sharply corniced ridges. Christjan indicated an area that was safe for skiing, well away from the potential trajectory of a falling cornice that was created by high winds streaming over the ridge tops. Off he went, faster now and skiing like a dream. My entire group was a dream group—and considerate. They knew it was my first day and wanted to give me all the encouragement they could. One of the prime positions in heli-skiing is to follow immediately after the guide. This is the best chance to ski untracked snow. My fellow skiers gave me the nod, more than was my fair share, to head out first. This was one of those runs.

Skiing in deep snow is rhythmic—at least it's supposed to be. When I was able to match Christjan's track, turn for turn, I immediately fell into a wonderful beat. With snow flying up around me, I floated from one turn to the next. The slope was not evenly steep so, as I progressed down it, I had to adjust the curvature of my turns in order to stay in control and keep my speed down.

Even though the clouds were lifting and the sun was caressing our faces, the temperature was dropping to a chilly 10°F. This was good news indeed because every drop in degree actually assisted the snow in evaporating the trapped moisture, therefore improving its quality. This magical transformation of existing snow into something resembling newly fallen snow is part of what makes snow science so fascinating—especially for a skier. The snow became lighter and was easier to turn in—plumes of feathery white flew from each carved edge. It was exhilarating, addictive, like what I imagine dancing the tango must be.

Unfortunately we had to stop for lunch. I was surprised to learn that we didn't have to go back to the lodge, but had only to reconvene at the bottom of a run that was tucked in among the towering spruce trees. The helicopter arrived with urns of hot soup and tea, sandwiches, and freshly baked cookies. Luxury! A hot lunch! Somehow the guides had figured out how to have all four groups ski down from our various runs to the same spot for lunch. I don't know how this happened because we didn't appear to be skiing anywhere near each other. As they explained it, a number of runs funneled into the same pickup, and that's where they scheduled the ski groups to be just before lunch. There was a lot more coordination going on here than immediately met the eye—the area had 150 runs available over 579 square miles and elevations ranging from

900 feet to 10,168 feet—and yet we all ended up in the same small opening in the trees for lunch!

The complexity of the guides' work only increased as the day wore on and weary skiers from each of the groups began to trickle back to the lodge. This was not a matter of simply slipping off down a run and skiing into the lodge. This was a logistical high-wire act that appeared to require the combined savvy of the pilot and all four guides. Coordinating two skiers from group one, three skiers from group three, and so on, to be in the helicopter at the same time that it was returning to the lodge for refuelling was amazing to watch.

The groups became smaller and smaller. Eventually our group absorbed half of group one. As the helicopter had

fewer groups to service, we suddenly had more of its attention. The result? We skied more. Instead of dropping into a 2,000-foot run in 15 minutes, followed by a 5-minute wait for the helicopter, followed by a 5-minute ride, we skied the runs in 7 minutes, jumped into a waiting helicopter, and then the 5-minute ride seemed shorter. As the pace increased, we were skiing ourselves into a frenzy—but what an incredible frenzy. The sun beamed brightly and the visibility was fabulous. Sharp granite ridges, heavily crevassed glaciers, pure white snowfields, dark spruce forests,

Specially designed "fat boy" skis carve through deep, light snow, wind crust, sun crust, and changeable snow conditions with equal ease due to their flexibility, width, and flotation design.

Ammonium nitrate explosives can be
dropped from helicopters to shake loose
unstable snow before it can fall and bury
unwary skiers.

FOLLOW YOUR HEART

Creator of heli-skiing, Hans Gmoser, and his wife, Margaret, pause before heading down a run.

HELI-SKIING BEGAN IN THE MID-'60s, WHEN HANS GMOSER CAME UP WITH A NEW WAY TO ski remote mountain areas. Gmoser was born in 1932 in Traun, Austria. When he was 13, a priest cajoled his village to donate food so he could take 20 kids to a mountain hut for a week of skiing. Hans was among that group, and after that, mountains became his passion.

In 1951, Hans agreed to join his friend Leo Grillmair and move to Canada. There he became an entrepreneur in the outdoor industry—by 1957 Hans had his own mountain guiding company. He was continuing to climb more ambitious peaks and used his guiding business to take clients places he himself wanted to go. His accomplishments eventually brought him recognition. The second ascent of Mount Logan's East Ridge in 1959, and the first ascent of Mount McKinley's Wickersham Wall in 1963 cemented his reputation. He took people high into the Rocky Mountains on ski mountaineering trips. This involved hours of trekking up and often less than an hour of downhill skiing. He was also involved with film projects that allowed him to use fixed-wing planes and helicopters to scout locations.

In the mid-'60s all of these elements came together when Hans realized he might be able to take clients into the mountains using a helicopter. It was in the spring of 1965 that he tried this outrageous idea in the Bugaboos. The first flight was to the top of Bugaboo Glacier on a blazingly clear morning—arrival time was 7 a.m. On a ski tour, you would still be far down in the valley so early in the morning, but to be up among the peaks at sunrise, with the entire day and seemingly the entire world beneath your feet—well, that clinched it for him.

Ask Hans about his vision in those early days, and his response is, "I didn't really have a vision. We just wanted to ski more terrain."

everything was perfectly in view, and we just kept moving through it. Our pace quickened and the bumps and rolls and trees came at me faster and faster, and my muscles strained to keep up with my sheer gluttony for turns.

I kept thinking it was over and then Christjan would challenge us: Do you want another run? Yes! Finally, by 5 p.m., I craved the massage that was booked for me back at the lodge. Christjan even radioed ahead to let the masseuse know I'd be a bit late, but to hold the spot. We were headed on our last—and 17th—run of the day. After thousands of turns and too many close calls when I thought I was going to fall, the muscles in my legs and feet were screaming for relief. But what a wonderful feeling. Breathing the cold, clear air, inhaling and exhaling in sync with each turn, had stretched my lungs to their capacity. The high elevation sunlight and biting breeze had brushed my face with a rosy-hued glow. Dropping over steep rolls and floating through the big timber had taken all of the concentration and coordination that I could muster. Yes, my legs were tired, but I didn't care. It was what I had come for, and I was euphoric. The grin on my face was so broad that my lips were cracking.

We were the last group to return to the lodge. Everyone called us hard-core, and I was just about to bask in the attention, when I realized I had to rush down to my massage. Inka Nagy, the massage therapist, reassured me that I had only missed a few minutes of my time but that I'd better hustle my butt onto the table. I wasn't ready for Inka. She looks like a classic Norwegian—tall and blonde and beautiful, maybe even a little fragile. Not so. She waded into my quads, and I was howling in the first few minutes. "Oh," she said, "there appears to be a little toxin build-up there. We shall have to work it out."

Forty minutes later I staggered up to the bar for a well-earned glass of champagne. We toasted the safe return of the two skiers who had left the traverse line, and in return they congratulated me on my first day of heli-skiing. We were a jovial group. As we dove into our scrumptious meal of stuffed smoked salmon and freshly baked rolls, followed by roasted chicken with morel sauce, then a light lemony cheesecake and good strong coffee, the stories flowed. I was intrigued with the simplicity of the lodge scene, which I imagined my high-powered companions were not accustomed to. The ambience of the lodge was that of solid comfort— sturdy tables, intimidating stone fireplace, comfortable couches, good beds, down comforters, but nowhere did I see any hint of luxury. The scale of rooms was modest. My single bed was truly single. The bathroom was functional. The food was absolutely fresh and delicious, with nothing nouveau about it. Everything screamed quality, but without excess. I asked Hans, "Do your guests mind not having certain conveniences when they are so obviously accustomed to them?"

"No," he said. "For the most part they don't miss it at all. Neither do they miss the lack of phones, faxes, televisions, and Muzak." He went on to explain that if they did, he usually

The helicopter, with ski baskets that can carry gear and also aid landing in deep snow, ferries skiers back to the lodge.

encouraged them to think of alternatives for their vacation because, in his mind and for his heli-skiing operation, excess was not appropriate in the mountains.

Hans came from humble beginnings and his personal style is also understated. Yet he exudes a quiet confidence and aura of always being in the right place. He seems to have a sense of the world

for decades. Hans counts these friendships as some of the most valuable of all his experiences in the mountains.

As dinner ended and the stories wound down, we migrated back to the living room, reluctant to retire just yet. Hans disappeared briefly and returned with a zither. Two young Austrians joined him with a guitar and accordion, and soon the lodge was filled with Tyrolean beer-drinking songs (at least that's what they sounded like). Where did everyone learn to yodel! Rhythmic sounds, mountain songs, ribald words from time to time, people enjoying people, entertaining themselves—it was wonderful. I could sense Hans's strong connection to the mountains of his youth as he belted out song after song in an Austrian mountain dialect.

It was obvious that our respect for each other was mutual. We were all aware of the privilege of being in our surroundings, experiencing the joy of movement, the inspiration of being in high mountains, and the energy absorbed from others with the same passion.

I finally toddled off to bed, eager to rest my weary limbs and catch up on all that lost sleep. With the sounds of yodeling fading in my ears, my heli-stress dissipated.

The next few days were sheer joy, much like the first day, but with a deeper appreciation of this wild and wonderful sport. My trip progressed from anxious anticipation to the dream of a lifetime.

and of his natural role within it. Through his work, he has met people from a different social strata than what he was born to. Rich, famous, titled, and royal guests have come through the CMH doors. And because they experienced the mountains with Hans and his staff in such profound ways, they developed bonds that produced friendships lasting

Evening descends on the granite spires of
the Bugaboos in the area where heli-skiing
began nearly 40 years ago.

During a three-day llama trek in the Teton Range, hikers cross a meadow of lupine and cow parsnip in Wyoming's Jedediah Smith Wilderness Area.

TETON

CHAPTER TWO

ESCAPE

BY JOHN A. MURRAY / PHOTOGRAPHS BY BETH WALD

RETURNING to the Tetons is like coming back to the sea, or visiting a childhood home after a long absence. The roads wind through dark woods and sunny clearings and always there is the expectancy of the view at the farthest bend. At night, thunderstorms frequently awaken you from sleep, and you listen to the thunder and to the rain falling on the tent. In the morning, the clouds dissipate rapidly in the dry air and by nine or ten it is clear and you gaze at the great purple range as if it is some mythical Shangri-la. Birds sing in the high groves of aspen and fir. Some make a song like a mandolin being tuned and others produce a melody like wind chimes tinkling in the breeze. Downy woodpeckers can sometimes be heard thumping in the trees, and the pine squirrels are alert sentries for their neighborhoods. The Teton Range is part of the Rocky Mountains extending through northwestern Wyoming, to southeastern Idaho. It is best visited in summer when the burning sun scorches the lower country, for that sort of heat never reaches the mountains' heights. The magic of the high range settles like a fine yellow pollen on all who visit, from the legendary painter, Thomas Moran (1837-1926), to photographer Ansel Adams (1902-1984).

LEFT / Switchbacks allow hikers and llamas to descend the north side of Green Mountain, where animals such as hawks, coyotes, and bears can often be seen. ABOVE / Indian paintbrush ranges in color from yellow-green to brilliant scarlet. Semi-parasitic, it can penetrate the roots of neighboring plants for additional food.

My most recent trip to the west side of the Teton Range began on a sunny day in mid-July. The fireweed was just beginning to blossom—bright lavender racemes set atop tall stems—and beside the streams the huckleberry plants were covered with pinkish-white blossoms. Everywhere there was the scent of flowers. It was late in the day and my 12-year-old son, Steven, and I were following a gravel road along Wyoming's Leigh Creek. In this big, wild country and we drove for miles without seeing any other vehicles. There were stands of conifer, groves of quaking aspen and, every once in a while, a clearing filled with blue larkspur and yellow arnica.

At one point a doe and two fawns appeared at the side of the road. I stopped the car, turned off the engine, and let them cross undisturbed by our presence. The twins still had black and white spots, and they moved playfully around their vigilant mother.

A short while later I turned onto a road that was more rugged than where we found the deer, and soon we entered a remote corner of the Targhee National Forest. Steven, reading from a forest service map, said that the forest was named for a Bannock chief killed by Crow Indians in the winter of 1871-72. He explained that the primary function of the forest was to protect the headwaters of the Snake River in western Wyoming and eastern Idaho. Scattered like jewels across the 1.8-million-acre forest were a number of roadless sanctuaries. Our destination that day was one of those—the Jedediah Smith

Wilderness Area. As we drove along, I explained to Steven that Jedediah Smith was one of the pioneering explorers of the Old West. He was a fur trapper turned geographer who roamed the frontier after explorers Lewis and Clark opened the West in the early 1800s.

Several miles farther, the road ended in a rolling grassy park about the size of a football field. It was there that Steven and I stopped to make camp for the night. We were excited, for the next morning we would begin a llama trip into the backcountry. For 30 years I had hiked the trails of the Teton Range on the eastern front, north of Jackson, Wyoming. Now I would have the opportunity to become acquainted with the western side of the Tetons. It was my first trip to this particular location, and I was with my son, so we would have the chance to explore a terra incognita together—and, as I found out later, learn a lot about llamas.

After setting up the tent and gathering firewood, we explored our new residence for the evening. A placard on a log fence explained that the surrounding meadow was the site of the Hill Sawmill, which had operated continuously from 1921 to 1976. After its closure, the forest service dammed a spring and created a marsh across the mill grounds to help various at-risk species. This wetland was now a breeding area for spotted frogs, tiger salamanders, western toads, and chorus frogs. The central pond was ringed with beaked sedge and cattails. At a distance, the fence kept the occasional visiting

range cattle and trail horses out. In the surrounding trees there was a bustling community of goldfinches and bluebirds. Sometimes their calls rang out—trills and twitters and soft warbles. Other times the birds flashed by, a sudden bit of color at vision's edge.

After dinner, Steven tried fishing the pools of North Leigh Creek above camp. The brook trout were plainly visible as slender darting shadows among the rocks, but they could not be enticed by any manner of dry or wet fly. I sat against a tree and watched my son fish in silence, marveling at how the eight-pound, five-ounce newborn the delivery nurse had handed me yesterday had suddenly been transformed into a big-shouldered young man with a cheerful personality and boundless curiosity.

Dusk came—by the time the last hermit thrush song came at 9:45 p.m., the fire was low and the stars were thick.

Sometime during the night it rained. During the deluge one of us—I forget which—slept peacefully. The other dashed outside the tent to adjust the fly.

The next morning, the first visitors at the trailhead were horse packer J.C. Stimson and forest service ecologist Chad Kashmier. The two were en route to a site on the Teton Crest, where they would inventory the alpine plants and trees growing there. They would then return at

Before leaving camp at Green Lakes, outfitter Dave Hodges holds the lead of a llama named Gil while his colleagues balance and adjust the panniers. The loads are carefully measured to weigh between 50 to 60 pounds.

intervals to evaluate changes in the plants' health and growth rate at the sample locations. This was part of an extensive program to keep a close watch on the health of plant life in the national forests.

Green Mountain's serried cliffs glow at sunset while storm clouds veil Idaho's distant valleys and mountains.

J.C.—who resembled the late cowboy-actor Richard Farnsworth—noted that the night rain had already been completely absorbed into the bone-dry ground. Concerned, he shook his head at the forest's dry condition. (One week later, a 4,500-acre forest fire would sweep across the Tetons near Jackson.) As the pair rode off into the

Jackson Hole Llamas for about a decade. They love sharing their favorite places in the high country with kindred souls each summer. With them were Brandon Cunningham, a 36-year-old police officer for the town of Jackson, and Suzanne Knighton, a 23-year-old intern with the Jackson Hole Conservation Alliance. A third-generation native of Wyoming, Brandon was named for the child actor in the classic Western movie *Shane*, which was filmed in Jackson in 1952. Suzanne was a true wilderness aficionado—we soon learned that she had recently climbed Mount Kilimanjaro and explored the upper reaches of the Amazon River.

Also along for the trip was Beth Wald, a photographer who would become the hardest-working member of the group, forever striving to capture the heart of the Teton Range on film.

Once the llamas were tied to the fence, we began preparations for our three-day journey. It would take us 18 miles along the Green Lakes Trail as we would weave our way deep into the Jedediah Smith Wilderness Area, hike to a view of the Grand Teton, and loop back. We brushed the llamas, saddled them with wooden pack saddles, and loaded them with panniers. Jill weighed each canvas pannier on a hand-held scale. A llama can carry as much as 80 pounds, but Jill made sure to give them a load that weighed a less. Then, like an attentive mother, she carefully distributed the individually tailored loads

high country, I thought of all the rush-hour traffic jams in distant cities and how fortunate these two men were to be riding to work on trail horses.

Shortly thereafter, Dave Hodges and his wife, Jill, arrived with a livestock trailer full of llamas. Dave and Jill, both in their 40s but with the kinetic energy of 20-year-olds, have operated among her nine "children." The llamas were lovely animals, with long eyelashes, bulging eyes, erect mobile ears, and overhanging, deeply cleft lips (they have no upper teeth). They weighed around 350 pounds each and ranged in color from reddish brown to sandy white. Most were a pinto combination of the two. The llamas communicated in soft braying voices that almost resembled a hum. It seemed related to the language of goats and sheep.

Soon we were on the trail, switch-backing up through the sage meadows and spruce groves. My son led a llama named Buster. I held the lead rope to Buster's best friend, Frito. Both were a burnt umber color, although Frito had a white blaze on his nose that distin-guished him from Buster. The llamas proved easy to lead—somewhat like leading an old dog. We learned that llamas love to sample vegetation—bark, twigs, branches, pinecones, leaves, flowers, even lichens. I could see that llamas, being browsers, would cause less damage to the environment than horses and mules, which tend to feed primarily on one food source—grass. Llamas also have two-toed feet, with soft pads like a camel's, and are consequently more gentle on trails than horses or mules.

It being July, the flowers were at their peak of bloom. The wild gardens presented an amazing spectacle. As we hiked along, I began to maintain an inventory in my field notebook—and soon grew short of pages: Yellow balsamroot, mountain gentian, white columbine, and horsemint were among my favorites. But there were also wild roses, monkshood, and rabbitbrush.

The lower meadows also supported an array of migratory songbirds. Chief among these, in sheer beauty, was the horned lark with black stripes under its eyes and small horns of black feathers. It was impossible for me to have cloudy feelings as it called *tsee-ee* or *tsee-titi*—even when one of the llamas sat down in the middle of the trail and refused to move until it had completed its meditations.

As we waited, I explained to Steven that the horned lark is in the lark fami-ly, unlike the meadowlark (state bird of Wyoming), which is a member of the blackbird family. The horned lark is a year-round resident of its birthplace. As a result, each local population adapts to the color of its habitat. Only once, after resuming the hike, did we glimpse one of these cheerful troubadours. As its song echoed across the mountainside while it flew, I thought of Shakespeare's sonnet: "Haply I think on thee,—and then my state,/Like to the lark at break of day arising/From sullen earth, sings hymns at heaven's gate."

Upward we climbed, all 16 of us—the nine llamas included. The trail at times cut back and forth across pitched slopes and on other occasions followed a natural contour line across the terrain. Gradually the alpine peaks—nearly bereft of snow—were coming into view. Behind us the valleys were sinking away.

WILDFLOWERS

Blue gentians begin to bloom in late July and continue flowering well into September.

MORE THAN 1,100 SPECIES OF VASCULAR PLANTS AND 7 SPECIES OF CONIFEROUS TREES grow in the Greater Yellowstone Ecosystem. Of these, the most abundant in the high alpine areas are the wildflowers. These native flowers are often divided by color in field guides—white, red-pink, yellow, and blue-purple. Among the white flowers, some of the most beautiful are the marsh marigold, which is found in wet meadows, and the spring beauty, which blossoms with delicate, pink veins as early as April on hillsides in clusters with other plants.

Although few people ever see them, a most striking red-pink flower is the rare calypso orchid; a stunning velvet red, it blossoms in June. Another perennial favorite in this color group is the wild rose, which produces an edible fruit that is rich in Vitamin C. The blossom of the red monkeyflower—which resembles that of the snapdragon or an orchid—is one of the most distinctive in the Teton Range. Toward the end of the flowering season, the pink petals drop into streams, painting the surface of the water with bright color. The plant favors locations near the water where the soil is usually deep and rich with nutrients.

Yellow flowers are striking against a blue sky, whether in the higher elevations—the yellow monkeyflower and alpine cinquefoil—or at lower elevations—the prickly pear cactus and rabbitbrush. Indian paintbrush, with between 150 and 200 species in North America, is commonly found in Wyoming and is in fact the state flower.

Blue-purple flowers include two species with poisonous plants—monkshood, also known as wolfsbane, and larkspur. Both plants have analgesic or anti-inflammatory properties, but eating their roots or leaves may cause paralysis of the cardiac and respirator centers However, the plants are rarely a problem, for cattle or people, in the national forest.

Littles Peak's summit ridge above Leigh Canyon rewards Dave Hodges and Brandon Cunningham with a stunning vista of Mount Moran (left) and Mount Woodring (right).

The air was noticeably cooler in the heights and it seemed from the less developed state of the flowers—buds instead of blossoms—that we were marching back into spring. At one point Dave observed that a bit of the Montana mountains—a pair of pale purple peaks—had come into view to the north. To the west rolling wheat fields and the far ranges of Idaho filled the horizon.

At one o'clock, after hiking around 4.5 miles, we stopped on a shoulder of Green Mountain, which stands at 9,614 feet, and had lunch overlooking the headwaters of North Leigh Creek. We sat just out of the

Steven, Brandon, and Jill settle into an afternoon game of Scrabble at their camp at Green Lakes in the Jedediah Smith Wilderness of Targhee National Forest.

wind, feasting on turkey and cheese sandwiches that Jill prepared while we admired the view. The headwaters formed a thousand-foot-deep canyon, and the sides were covered in old growth timber and talus slopes. The canyon appeared an ideal place for a grizzly bear sow and her cubs to spend the summer in peaceful obscurity. All around us a flock of violet-green swallows dipped and swerved on bent wings as they feasted upon wind-blown mosquitoes. Their seasonal nests could be seen in the cliffs on the north side of Green Mountain.

At one point Dave motioned to a place called Dry Ridge across the canyon, where a cross-country skier had been killed in an avalanche the previous winter. He said that a melted area had been found around the victim's head, indicating she had been able to breathe for some time before suffocating.

After awhile we gathered our things and resumed the journey. A little after four, our expedition arrived at the high camp, having hiked about seven miles and climbed up about 2,300 feet. It was the first outing of the year for the llamas, and so we had taken it slow—which was fine with me. Our climbs, although mostly on gentle slopes, required hours of exertion and careful attention so as not to stumble. My legs became sore.

The campsite was located on a grassy knoll above a small, unnamed lake. Behind the lake was a timbered ridge and beyond that ridge was the gray-blue summit of Littles Peak. Our first job was to unsaddle the llamas and give them water. Dave and Jill were the sergeants in this enterprise, and the rest of us were the privates, carefully following instructions. We picketed six of the nine llamas, but left the others to roam. Being social animals, the untethered llamas remained close to their companions.

We humans then dispersed with tents under arm. Steven and I raised ours in a secluded nook about 30 yards from the cook tent. It was a perfect place—flat and free of rocks and naturally protected by subalpine trees. There was even a waterfall down the hill to provide the white noise conducive to sleep.

Dinner, prepared by our accomplished backcountry chef Jill, followed shortly—tossed salad, farfalle pasta in marinara sauce with Italian sausage and garlic bread, followed by a dessert of shortbread cookies.

At night by the campfire, we saw brilliant stars. The Milky Way stretched across the sky, its ancient form radiant with grottoes and dark gulfs. To the east, Littles Peak, our destination for the next day's hike, glowed as if beneath a fluorescent light. No artist—not even Frederic Remington—has ever fully captured the beauty of the western night.

As we drifted off to sleep I thought of Jedediah Smith, and how this wild area honored the best of his life— that quintessential American spirit of adventure and optimism and generosity. A calm, devout man, he led expeditions into unknown areas of the West in the 1800s. He remained steadfast and determined—despite setbacks that included getting mauled by a bear and suffering temperatures so hot that he and his men had to bury themselves in the sand until the mercury dropped.

I closed my eyes. The last thing I heard was the hoot of an owl.

IN THE mountains, all trails eventually lead to the high peaks. They beckon to us from afar and rise with prominence from lower ridges. They offer a ladder to the sky and a vision of the world below. They are older than the rivers, and they are covered with the scars of their antiquity. They are eminences before they are anything else, and in the literal sense of that word.

The Tetons have a particularly strong presence in this respect, rising as they do nearly a mile in the sky above the Snake River Valley north of Jackson. Wherever they occur, the high peaks tend to rise in groups that resemble families. You can almost discern family members by their various characteristics—towering patriarchs and beautiful matriarchs, eldest sons and daughters with a strong resemblance to the larger peaks, but not as geologically old.

I was thinking about all this the next morning as we breakfasted and listened to Dave describe the route we would take up Littles Peak, which is a distant nephew to Mount Moran. The day had dawned bright and clear, and conditions were ideal for the climb. Everyone was looking forward to the trek.

Shortly after ten we set off up the trail, led, as always, by Toby, the Hodges' golden retriever-mix (formerly a resident of the town pound). The trail followed the eastern shore of the lake, where hoary marmots whistled indignantly and Toby barked inquisitively. Then it crossed a meadow and began climbing the near ridge. Halfway up we stopped to rest and look back toward camp, where Suzanne had remained to care for the llamas. By then the camp was lost in the trees.

On top of the ridge, Jill and I lingered for a moment to study fur-filled scat on the trail. It seemed too large for a coyote and too small for a bear. Jill wondered if, based on size, it might be a wolf, a

species reintroduced into the Greater Yellowstone Ecosystem in 1995. Wolves have dispersed from their new home in Yellowstone National Park, and are now found in the Tetons and Wind River Range to the south. They have proven an economic boom to local counties, as wildlife lovers flock to wolf-watch at all seasons of the year.

Soon we left the formal trail and headed cross-country over the tundra toward a low saddle just north of Littles Peak. The meadows were filled with vast constellations of white bistort and yellow glacier lily, both favored summer food of grizzly bears. Bluebells and Indian paintbrush grew in profusion wherever there were springs or alpine streams.

Periodically the chirps of alarmed pikas filled the air.

Half an hour later we found ourselves at the base of Littles Peak. The view in

Towering at 13,770 feet, the west face of the Grand Teton basks in the sun. Most climbers approach the peak from the south rather than tackling the more difficult route on the north face.

Llama trekkers tell stories by the campfire. To minimize any damage to the ecosystem, all fires are built in metal pans and the ashes are packed up and carried out.

LLAMA LIFE

A llama is tethered for the night where it can still graze.

THE THREE SPECIES OF LLAMAS ORIGINATED IN SOUTH AMERICA. THEY ARE THE GUANACO (*Llama guanaco*), llama (*Llama glama*), and alpaca (*Llama pacos*)—and their cousin, the vicuña (*Vicugna vicugna*). They differ from camels, which are their nearest relatives, in that they are much smaller and have no dorsal humps. In the wild, llamas live in family herds composed of a breeding male, several females, and young of various ages. They frequent the uplands during the rainy season, and move onto the plains when it is dry.

Llamas are well-adapted to life in the high mountains and, with their thick, multi-layered fur, are comfortable in all types of weather. They spend much of their time resting by kneeling (a position called "cush" by llama owners), and ruminating undigested food through their three stomachs. Often they enjoy a good wallow in the dirt. It has been theorized that this could be related to territorial scent marking.

When alarmed, llamas let out a bleat similar to that of a deer or an elk. At this signal the females drive the young before them, while the male acts as a guard to protect the herd. During the mating season the males engage in violent contests, and the young are born to the females 11 months later. Males without females live in bachelor bands.

Llamas and alpacas are domestic animals used by indigenous people of the Andes. Male llamas are used as pack animals while alpacas are raised for their wool, which is used in weaving. Vicuñas, once hunted for their meat, and guanacos, live free in the high Andes. Llamas are increasingly popular in the Rocky Mountains because their two-toed, padded feet are more gentle on the environment than the larger, hard hooves of other pack animals such as horses and mules. They are also more easily handled by children.

every direction was incredible. To the east was a U-shaped glacial valley in Grand Teton National Park (the park was everything east of our position on the Teton Crest). Far to the east a bit of Spalding Bay on Jackson Lake near Moran Junction was visible between two lower canyon walls. The northeastern horizon was dominated by the backside of Mount Moran. I had never seen Moran from the western vantage, and noted that the black dike on the summit that is so striking from the east runs completely through the top of the peak. To our north was an array of alpine peaks as sharp as the canine teeth of a young wolf. To the west the mountains sloped down to the plains of Idaho, which were spread as flat and calm as a pale-blue morning sea.

Littles Peak was now fully in view along the Teton Crest to the south. Although it appeared to be a fairly gentle mountain from the western approach—something like an eroded pyramid—the east side of the mountain consisted of a series of abrupt cliffs and talus slopes. Despite the lateness of the season, snowbanks lingered in some of these deeply shaded hollows. Beyond a ridge east of Littles Peak we could see the top of the Grand Teton (newly dusted with snow) and Mount Owen.

Jill and Dave quickly prepared lunch—bagels and cream cheese that were followed by fruit and cookies—which we passed around the circle. Then we rested a few minutes in the sun before embarking on the climb.

While Steven and Jill remained behind, Beth, Dave, Brandon, and I set out for the peak. Although I hated to leave Steven behind, I considered the climb too steep and dangerous for him. The most natural route followed the eastern cliff rim and involved some bouldering. Occasionally, like climbing a jungle gym as a child, I went hand-over-hand past a tumble of a few house-size rocks. During the ascent I often heard the warning clucks of rock ptarmigan, and once I spotted a single bird sitting on top of a nearby boulder. It was a male, with the distinctive red comb over the eye. He wore his dull summer plumage—brown and gray and black—and had a few white feathers on his chest remaining from the previous winter.

Within sight of the summit I heard a faint "Hey Dad!" on the wind and turned to wave and yell back toward my son. Although Steven and Jill were half a mile away and appeared as two specks of color on the tundra, I knew that they were observing our progress with binoculars.

I reached the top (10,721 feet) some time before the others, who had lingered to take photographs. The summit—literally a pile of rocks—provided a broad prospect of the central Tetons. The view was that of the red-tailed hawk or the golden eagle. All around, granite peaks lifted toward the cobalt blue sky—from Table Mountain on the south (where actor and Jackson resident Harrison Ford had found a young couple in his helicopter the previous summer) to Window Peak on the north (marking the head of Moran Canyon). The view to the south was of considerable interest to me, as I had often hiked up Paintbrush Canyon to Solitude Lake on earlier trips. In fact, it was in Paintbrush Canyon that I had first hiked in the Tetons three decades earlier.

For many minutes I pondered the passage of time, as well as the procession of events both personal and cultural since that first experience. Mountaintops have long been places of epiphany—from the days of Moses to Tenzing and Hillary's ascent of Everest—and Littles Peak that day was no different. I was reminded again that we climb not to conquer, but to be conquered, to be in the presence of an entity that invigorates and inspires even as it exhausts. I saw, too, that Littles Peak has a spirit, like a man or a woman or a child. The mass of rock, the angle of the slopes, the life that prospers here— all combine to form an entity as real and palpable as any other on Earth. It rises, as we do, from the Earth and reaches always for the sky. If the peak revealed one certainty to me that day, it was that time is not endless and that nothing is made in earnest. We come to such places much as pilgrims—for revelation as well as for recreation.

I carried from the place an ordinary stone no larger than my thumb. It was a gift for my son.

Back at the staging area (the descent taking roughly a third of the time of the

ascent), I rejoined Jill to hear the story of how she and Dave met 20 years earlier while planting trees for the forest service. They then moved to Jackson, where Dave worked as an instructor for the National Outdoor Leadership School before becoming a deputy sheriff, and Jill worked as a massage therapist. They had owned llamas for about ten years.

Over time their 18 llamas had become their family.

Eventually the others returned, and we retraced our steps the two miles back to camp, each grateful for the opportunity to have wandered along the Teton Crest on such a sunny, wonderful day.

Sometime after seven, as Jill finished preparing dinner in the cook tent, an immense purple-black cloud began to form over the peaks. We anticipated only the daily rains that are common in the

One of the many Green Lakes reflects blue skies in the Teton Range. Hoary marmots inhabit the rocks next to the pond. There they have built complex tunnel systems that connect shelters, nurseries, and food storage areas.

mountains during the summer, but Mother Nature had a surprise for us. Just as we began to dine upon stir-fried chicken and rice, a violent hailstorm swept in and scattered everyone to their tents. The storm that followed was like something from the weather-stained journals of Jedediah Smith—incandescent flashes of lightning, artillery-like explosions of thunder, sudden gusts of wind that nearly flattened the tent, and tremendous torrents of hail and rain.

Fifteen minutes later, so typical in the high mountains, the skies were

Hikers pause on Green Lakes Trail to admire the view. The plains of Idaho stretch beyond lush grass meadows where elk and deer can often be found grazing in the morning and evening hours.

completely clear and we gathered around the fire for the traditional evening pastime of all campers: storytelling. Our stories ranged from the personal to the historic. Brandon provided a fascinating account of the Golden Age of filmmaking in Jackson—from a young unknown actor named John Wayne in *The Big Trail* (1930) to Kirk Douglas in *The Big Sky* (1951) and Henry Fonda in *Spencer's Mountain* (1963). He related how half-wild buffalo herds were brought in for scenes in *The Big Trail*, and how the raft with Kirk Douglas nearly tipped over in the Snake River. *Spencer's Mountain* was shot at the Triangle X dude ranch just south of Moran Junction on U.S. Route 89.

These stories reminded us of how powerful landscape can be—places such as the Tetons—in creating and nurturing popular myths and heroes.

EVERY journey must have its final day. Ours began comically, on day three, with Beth opening our tent flap shortly after sunrise and taking photos when Steven and I were defenseless and looking our worst—half-opened eyes, unwashed faces, bad hat-head. Still in our sleeping bags, we squirmed like two coyote pups. We were good sports, however, and cheerfully helped the photographer as best we could.

After a quick breakfast of oatmeal and fruit, everyone scattered over the knoll and began breaking camp—packing the tents and gear, rounding up the llamas, and securing the saddles and panniers.

Somehow this process took only about one hour. Having worked as a horse wrangler on Colorado and Wyoming ranches in my youth, I was continually amazed at how easy it was to work with llamas—no dangerous rodeos, no Herculean efforts, just a simple partnership with a patient animal that seemed to have both intelligence and grace.

Upon our departure, Dave announced that we would be taking a "Wyoming Trail" off the mountain as a kind of short cut, and urged us to be alert to the subtleties of the terrain. There would be dense forest, wandering game paths, talus slopes, stream crossings, and so forth. The path proved not that bad—just two rocky areas that required a slower pace—and within half an hour we were back on the major trail.

Dave then proclaimed that we had all earned our "official certificates of advanced llamaneering."

The rest of the descent was downhill—except for one ridge that required a brisk climb of some 14 switchbacks. Hiking out was a slow return to midsummer, both in the flowers (those budding above were in blossom below) and in the temperature (everyone began shedding sweaters and shirts).

Eventually the trailhead appeared, and then there was that sweet sadness that accompanies the end of a happy journey. We shook hands, embraced, took last photographs, and parted, knowing that we had made friends to whom we would return in the years to come, just as we would the Tetons.

For several miles Steven and I drove down the gravel road in silence, each reflecting upon the shared experience and returning through recollection to various moments and high points. Some trips come and go without note, and others are always cherished. It was becoming apparent that this trip—a father and son on a first-time adventure to the Tetons together—would be fondly remembered.

As we approached the paved highway, Steven turned for one final look at the range and exclaimed, much to his father's delight, "Dad, I think I have fallen in love with the Tetons!"

Sudden rain and hail hit the high country in the summer months when storms form around mountain peaks. Within 15 minutes of this cloudburst, the skies were clear and the rainbow gone.

DESERT
COMMUNION

CHAPTER THREE

BY ALLAN FALLOW / PHOTOGRAPHS BY PETER McBRIDE

HURTLING

down a dirt switchback in Utah's Canyonlands National Park, it occurs to me I'm in this thing way over my head.

Geologically I'm in over my head because the White Rim Trail—our loop route for the next four days and 100 miles of mountain biking—has plummeted 1,500 feet from the mesa top in our first 5.5 miles of riding.

Professionally, as a writer who's been on the beat almost 25 years, I'm in over my head because the wind-molded weirdnesses of stone towering on my right and dropping away on my left seem intent on eluding capture in words.

And personally I'm in over my head because I've rashly agreed to tour this wild corner of Utah with seven other riders who delight in playing hard-body

hammerheads to my marshmallow flat-lander. Although I crank out 200 miles a week on my road bike back home in Virginia, those asphalt miles cannot compare with the washboard ruts, slickrock, loose stones, and deep sand that await us on the White Rim Trail. Plus I've never really ridden a mountain bike.

But there's no turning back. Having tarried at the trailhead, drinking in the sunset-painted cliffs and ledges marching to the distant blue La Sal Mountains, I now find myself racing nightfall, skidding and jouncing down the Shafer Canyon switchbacks while a shred of daylight

LEFT / A slab of White Rim sandstone 250 feet thick dwarfs a quartet of riders below 5,865-foot-high Candlestick Tower. ABOVE / Cerulean skies and an easy trail grade ease the way to the Goose Neck.

remains in the sky. If I don't reach camp by dark, I risk breaking not only my neck but the vow I made to my wife, Mimi, that I would return from this adventure in one piece—preferably alive.

Riding beside me is Chip Davis, a curly-haired optimist who advises me to "get comfortable skidding." I squeeze my rear brake lever and practice sluing to a stop amid a ground-level hail of dust and pebbles on the 27-speed Rocky Mountain Spice I've rented for the week. The bike's dual suspension (shock absorbers front and rear) will prove essential.

The massive sandstone walls and alcoves that climb higher and higher above our heads are streaked with desert varnish —a mineral residue that glistens reddish-brown from iron oxide or lustrous black from manganese oxide.

For someone accustomed to the tamer scenery east of the Mississippi, such geologic grandeur quickly overloads the circuits: "Dang!" I confess to Elizabeth Hightower, a 34-year-old raven-haired amazon who is the literary editor of a nationally known outdoor magazine. "I didn't pack enough adjectives!"

I did pack "unfenced," "exposed," and "treacherous," however, all of which describe this cliffhanger of a trail, where a moment's inattention means a 1,000-foot freewheel to the canyon floor below. We keep our eyes peeled for wildlife, too, brought out by the cool of the evening. Gray-brown sagebrush lizards flee at our approach, while bats zigzag over our heads. Having decided that these vertiginous

environs must be the real-life home of Wile E. Coyote, we misidentify the birds that scamper before us as roadrunners (it turns out they're Gambel's quail).

A pair of Barbie and Ken look-alikes come bombing down the trail. Judging from their perfect pecs and specs, their chiseled bods and quads, they are models en route to a Gary Fisher Sugar mountain bike commercial.

Wrong.

They are 28-year-olds Katie Monahan and Matt Holstein, late arrivals to our group. Katie—a shy, buff speed specialist just back from training with the U.S. Ski Team in Chile—will turn out to be the strongest and most technically gifted cyclist in our group. Her tent mate Matt, a fastidious Aspen realtor, points to the desert floor below: "Look, you can start to see the White Rim down there."

Following his finger, I spy a nearly unbroken sandstone bench whose prominent white overhang makes it stand out from the chocolate-colored layers of rock stacked above and below it. Roughly paralleling its scalloped contours and running off into the desert across the floor of Shafer Canyon is the White Rim Trail— actually a road, since its twin tracks are navigable by four-wheel-drive vehicles.

Differential erosion of the hard White Rim sandstone and the softer Organ Rock shale beneath it has created Canyonlands' trademark formations: cliffs, canyons, mesas, buttes, fins, and arches, plus a thriving crop of freestanding stone pillars, monoliths, and spires.

This wild riot of colored rock draws an alarming number of admirers. Park visitorship, lamented writer Timothy Egan in 2001, grew sixfold from 1979 to 1999, when it hit 446,527. You'll have a hard time convincing me of that four days from now, by which time I will have encountered just three dozen fellow tourists. Indeed, the park's human population may even be declining. "Canyonlands received 401,558 visitors in 2000," interpretive ranger Katie Juenger informs me later on. "About 60 percent of them visited the Island in the Sky District, but only 6,242 requested White Rim permits."

I scoot back on the saddle—a tactic Chip taught me for controlled descent—and continue my plunge into the gloom. Do I mind eating the trail dust kicked up when Katie and Matt blow by me? Not a bit: I gratefully follow their billows to a trail split I would have missed in the dark. The left fork—the two-wheel-drive Potash Road—leads to Shafer Camp, our first desert bivouac. (With only 20 primitive campsites dotting the White Rim Trail, each overnight stop must be reserved through the park service months in advance.)

"Camp" is too grandiose a term for the Shafer site. It boasts an outhouse (as do all Canyonlands campsites) and by day it offers an untrammeled view—inspiring or daunting, depending on your direction of travel—of the stone wall we just descended. Beyond that it is nothing but a desolate bowl of rock,

Sunni Simpson—potter, massage therapist, goddess of camp cuisine—sports desert-cycling basics: helmet with visor, sunglasses, water supply.

floored with maroon shale and hemmed in by sheer walls of mud-colored flowstone.

Welcoming me to this stark serai is John McBride, a 36-year-old National Ski Team coach who is ripped to the brink of cyborg status. "Are those veins on your legs real," the others rib him, "or did you have them surgically applied?"

"Johno" has driven down the Shafer switchbacks ahead of us in our support vehicle: a four-wheel-drive pickup stuffed to its camper roof with sleeping bags and cooking gear, cases of food and coolers of beer—and enough water, I pray, to keep the eight of us alive in the baked terrain that lies ahead.

Setting up her tailgate *batterie de cuisine* is 28-year-old Sunni Simpson, a quiet but iron-willed blonde I will come to call the Steel Tumbleweed (but never in front of her fiancé, Johno). The last rider to roll into camp is Johno's younger brother, Pete McBride, a 30-year-old adventure-travel photographer.

The others don headlamps—don't attempt this trip without one—and bustle about camp. Elizabeth chops onions and carrots for a chicken stew. Chip and Matt troubleshoot the mantle on a white-gas lantern. Katie sets up her two-man Bibler. ("That's the most expensive tent out there," Matt informs us.) Pete positions his tripod to capture the moonrise, and Sunni fires up her stove to steam rice.

Soon we're in the thick of a full-on feed bag (if you want to ride with the wolves, you've got to talk like them), eight camp chairs circled around the

lantern glow. "Hunger is the best sauce," Chip remarks between forkfuls.

After a classy dessert of double-stuffed Oreos, we play a few rounds of desert braggadocio. The evening's most farcical fable finds Pete in an Ecuadoran hotel room at 4 a.m., trying to explain to an agitated American airline pilot how Pete came to occupy the same room as Mari-

leña, the South American dance instructor who can't choose between them.

Around 10 o'clock the moon clangs into the sky above the eastern horizon, bathing the canyon floor in brilliant metallic light. It reveals a campsite littered with prickly-pear cactus and sharp chips of shale—the kind guaranteed to dig into your back at 3 a.m. Then comes further illumination: Given the warm night air and the low likelihood of rain—Canyonlands receives just nine inches of annual precipitation—maybe I should have packed a sleeping pad instead

At the head of Little Bridge Canyon, a cyclist marvels at pillars of soft Organ Rock shale capped by hard White Rim sandstone.

of a tent (there was no room for both). Happily, three padded camp chairs laid end to end serve the purpose just as well.

About the site's pronounced incline, however, I can do nothing: I drift off to a Chip Davis monologue on "Doing the Desert Luge."

TWO A.M. and I'm wide awake, the crunch

of gravel beneath my sandals shattering the perfection of the silence. I feel electrified, energized, as though I've tapped into some primal life force the White Rim capstone is powerless to contain.

Morning light bathes the seemingly quarried walls of the Goose Neck—a bight in the Colorado River— and the sandstone layers rising above them.

Something similar may have been experienced on a June day 133 years ago by pioneering adventurer John Wesley Powell, the one-armed Civil War veteran who descended the Green River through Canyonlands in 1869 (95 years before 528 square miles of the area were designated the 32nd U.S. national park). Having shot his first set of river rapids, Powell confided to his journal, "I do not sleep for some time, as the excitement of the day has not worn off."

I'm spooked into returning to my sleeping bag by the conviction that the rocks looming overhead have come alive and resent my presence. (Why else would that cliff near camp resemble a terrifying toad?) Thus I'm a tad giddy to see the dawn. Most of the others roust early, too—a rarity for this bibulous bunch—and without pausing for breakfast we jump on our bikes and pedal off into the soft morning sunlight that is the best part of any desert day.

Our goal is the giant riverine coil known as the Goose Neck, two miles east of the park border on the Potash Road and 3.5 miles from camp. Here the Colorado unspools for four miles, passing southward within just 400 yards of its earlier north-flowing course. At this point in the river's path—35 miles upstream from its confluence with the Green—it flows between striated stone walls so perfectly sheer they seem chiseled by canal engineers.

The ride there is a downhill dream, and soon we're perched on the brink of a drop-off overlooking the Goose Neck. I'm immobilized less by acrophobia than by Johno's jokes about jumping. "Help, I can't get out of my clips!" he screams, rolling toward the cliff edge on his titanium Serotta hard tail (front suspension only), his cycling shoes apparently stuck in the pedals. At the last possible moment he clips out of them, aborting a fatal plunge—and bursting into a self-congratulatory cackle.

Oddly, the episode is a confidence builder: If I can tolerate the psychic tension of Johno's infatuation with the abyss, I console myself, I can easily survive whatever physical challenges the White Rim throws my way.

Back at camp, Elizabeth brews high-octane French-press coffee while Sunni doles out rations like a quartermaster:

"Don't take seconds on those scrambled eggs and sausage yet, Pete," she warns her future brother-in-law. "The Extreme Couple (Katie and Matt) haven't had breakfast yet."

"I'm just gonna have a whisper," he says, lurking and poaching.

Chip (Pete's college roommate, it emerged last night) isn't buying it: "That's McBride code for 'I'm eating the rest.'"

At midmorning, it's clear we're headed for a near-100-degree day. Edward Abbey captured the effect in *Desert Solitaire,* his blistering chronicle of the seasons he spent as a ranger at Arches National Monument next door: "The sun roars down from its track in space with a savage and holy light."

"So," says Chip, "I guess we're just in wither-and-die mode now, right?"

Wither-and-ride mode is more like it: I fill my two 32-ounce frame bottles and my 100-ounce Camelbak (a water-filled bladder in a backpack with a clear plastic tube leading to the wearer's mouth), clip into bike pedals fouled with red grit, and spin off through the contorted landscape. Pete dubs the surroundings "Dr. Seuss Land." (See *Horton Hears a Who!* for some close approximations.)

I ride easily along the level grade, gawking at the 3-D topography. Wedding cakes of rock soar above our heads or stairstep away beneath our feet. Far below, dry streambeds bristling with teetering rock towers snake their way downcanyon toward distant mountain ranges.

A time exposure captures both moonrise and star tracks over a Green River meander at Canyonlands' Labyrinth B campsite.

The day started out cloudless, but now a cumulus armada sails into the sky, teasing us with virga—shredded cascades of rain that evaporate before reaching the ground. Our elevation must still be fairly high, for dark green pinyon pines and Utah junipers—rarely seen below 4,500 feet—sprout from exposed hummocks of smooth, White Rim slickrock.

An hour or so later, at the Colorado River overlook known as the Walking Rocks, we cautiously crabwalk to the edge of the 900-foot-high precipice, then sit on its verge and dangle our legs over the side.

Cyclists break camp above "Frisbee Flats," a muddy playground near the Labyrinth B campsite on the east bank of the Green River. Bright green tamarisk trees line the waterway; Wingate walls and pillars create a rock amphitheater around it.

Jutting above the skyline in the middle foreground are impregnable walls and cathedral-shaped fortresses of Wingate sandstone, their reddish-brown sides rising to heights of 800 feet and more.

"Would you like to hear what John Wesley Powell had to say when he passed this way in 1869?" Elizabeth reads a passage that perfectly paints the scene upon which we are feasting: "Wherever we look there is but a wilderness of rocks—deep gorges where the rivers are lost below cliffs and towers and pinnacles, and ten thousand strangely carved forms in every direction, and beyond them mountains blending with the clouds."

"Damn," I mutter, "I'll *never* learn to write like a geologist!"

Pete's suffering no such qualms: "It's easy to use film out here, I tell ya!"

Our next port of call is Musselman Arch, a weathered gray rock span that is 50 feet long and 150 feet high but only four feet wide. Shaking my head at the idiocy (and illegality) of a stunt described in my guidebook—some bozos ride their bikes across the thing—I look up to see Sunni, Johno, and the Extreme Couple pulling synchronized handstands atop the storied span.

At the head of Little Bridge Canyon, we lay down our bikes and step across a six-inch-wide crack in the seemingly solid escarpment to grab a snack with a view. (Beef jerky and GU, anyone?) Like circus crockery balanced atop bamboo canes, giant plates of White Rim sandstone are held aloft on either side of our vantage point by slender brown columns of freestanding Organ Rock shale. Not until it's time to saddle up again does Pete point out that we've been sitting on an unanchored pillar of our own. At his invitation, I gaze down into that six-inch crack—a prospect I'd resisted before—and find not solid ground but thin air and oblivion. As Powell noted, "It is curious how a little obstacle becomes a great obstruction when a misstep would land a man in the bottom of a deep chasm."

As we continue to log high rpms in low humidity, the talk turns to personal hydration systems. "I've drunk one whole Camelbak already," Matt grouses, but he has hardly made a dent in his recommended daily allowance: Experts urge you to guzzle as much as 2.5 gallons of water per day when you walk or cycle Canyonlands.

High noon finds us hunkered down in the sparse shade offered by the truck, desperately seeking shelter from Abbey's "bright inferno in the sky." We choke PB&Js down dusty gullets and discuss our next adventure: a four-mile side trip down sandy Lathrop Canyon to a swimming spot (and decommissioned park campsite) on the Colorado.

I'm intrigued by a mention of Appropriate Swimwear. "I'm wearing my one-piece," Elizabeth remarks.

"So am I," Katie replies. "The one-piece I wore on my birth day!"

Unlike the White Rim Trail—surveyed and built in the 1950s to provide access to supposedly rich uranium deposits—its side trails began as rutted, rocky, supersteep cattle tracks. So I shouldn't be surprised to find that the first serious incline on the descent of Lathrop Canyon is simply too precipitous to ride down. I unclip my right shoe, swing my leg over the saddle, and walk my Spice down the rutted pitch.

That hazard is nothing compared with trail sand. The trick is to ride into the sand with your front wheel perfectly straight, shift into a low gear, scoot your butt back on the seat, then spin, wallow, and fishtail your way to solid ground on the far side. It's a kick once you get the hang of it—a sensation akin to swimming on a bike—but your first attempts will most likely result in sandy spills.

At the end of this hard, hot slog is a priceless payoff: the sight of a great blue heron doing a John Cleese "silly walk" in the shallows by the river's far bank and—sweetest relief of all—the bliss and balm of swimming naked in what Abbey called the "brown, silt-rich bosom" of the Colorado.

For all its expanse, there's no room in the great Western wilderness for modesty: Johno has swum and waded to the tamarisk-infested opposite shore, where he lies starkers on his back. Younger brother Pete joins him and they wade upstream, knuckles dragging the surface of the water in a primordial tableau that my dehydrated brain captions "The Sasquatch Twins." Then Chip and Elizabeth join the procession, and I realize I'm witnessing an evolutionary step at the dawn of time.

Uninvited guests drop in on our idyll. A silver-haired couple glides downstream in a green canoe, the man profiting from his seat in the stern to scope out our wilderness Lorelei. It's a minor distraction compared with what comes next: Four Harley-throated jet skis roar into view, shattering the solitude in their haste to gain the Canyonlands border 7.5 miles upriver before a park ranger can bust them. Rooster tails of water and flatulent floccules of blue smoke chase them on their way; rainbow-colored oil slicks and the stench of incompletely burned fossil fuels linger in their wake.

Grinding back upcanyon, we take turns tackling the heinous final pitch, exhorting each other upward in lan-guage that reveals a generation gap wider than Lathrop Canyon itself. "Okay dude, get dialed in now," Chip psyches me up. "Bucky cadence, no bailing, now go, Go, GO!" Puzzling over what he just said occupies my mind long enough to get my body a third of the way up the 100-yard-long incline, but there I'm unhorsed by a technical issue: On grades this steep (and thus in gears this low) I pull my front wheel off the ground, sabotaging my advance.

The answer, Katie instructs me, is to balance your weight over the handlebars, pinning your front wheel to the ground. I try that, but my rear wheel spins out on the gravel. What's an asphalt habitué to do?

"You can drive the truck," Pete answers my unvoiced question. Each group member is expected to serve a stint behind the wheel, so I don't take it personally when we regain the White Rim bench and I find myself relieved of cycling for the evening.

Another lesson learned: Always navigate the sag wagon in the morning, when you can see what nasty surprises the terrain has in store. Manhandling the truck over boulders that would humble a Humvee, I watch sunset cloak the world in pre-moonrise murk. Three riders have pedaled ahead to the evening's campsite at Gooseberry A while four others have dropped off the back, casting me adrift in an alien world where twin cones of converging yellow light play over dark drop-offs to my left and scrubby

Martian flora to my right. The effect is so disorienting—and the rock cairns marking the route so erratic—that I convince myself I've lost the White Rim Trail altogether.

Looking hammered, the laggards eventually catch up. I refill everyone's water bottles, remarking on the rime of salt that encrusts Pete's riding togs, then stand aside while Sunni grieves for her steaks: The pummeling of the corrugated trail surface has ejected them from their ginger-cilantro marinade and into the melted ice at the bottom of the beer cooler.

Elizabeth, meanwhile, is ransacking the truck. Shouting "Pete's bonking!" she flings objects backward over both shoulders in a frantic quest to find a banana we can feed the photographer. Its high potassium content is a proven cramp-fighter.

Somehow we regain the trail and follow headlamps winking in the distance to a reunion at Gooseberry A, where Sunni's steak fajitas restore our strength and spirits. "Mmm, *love* this low-cal marinade," we carefully compliment the chef. Pete can't join the chorus; he's rolling in the dust in a fetal curl, suffering knife-jab sideaches from a day of too much photography and not enough hydration. I thank the water gods that I've been quaffing my daily ration.

By now our personal bubbles have shrunk to the point where Chip and I are on a shared-tarp basis. Before falling asleep, we observe a tradition that is all

Beside a sheer drop-off at Walking Rocks, the author tries to gather his belongings (and thoughts) after an intoxicating view of the distant La Sals.

Elizabeth Hightower (left) and Sunni Simpson swim in the cool and silty Green River. With 70 percent of the White Rim Trail paralleling desert waterways, such river dips are the payoff for parched pedaling.

of two days old: Each person recites the favorite and most forgettable moments of his or her day. In the former category, soothing our saddle sores with river water earns the most votes; in the latter it's a toss-up between the Lathrop Canyon climb and that final death march in the dark.

THE NEXT few days unreel in parched leisure, the bikes serving as ideal vehicles for discovering the desert and the Kids

Riders escape the sun beneath a rock overhang at the top of Holeman Slot Canyon. The indentations in the rock wall below the truck are *huecos,* or hollows; these smooth-sided pits show where wind erosion has gained a toehold in the rock.

granting me a tad more tribe-member status with every bone-jarring mile.

Johno, torn from slumber on Day 3 by a sky-streaked sunrise over the La Sals, raises his head from his sleeping bag just long enough to plead, "Will somebody please shut off that heat lamp in the sky?!" Jeez, Johno—by this hour I've brushed my teeth atop the canyon ledge, walked partway up the Gooseberry Trail (a three-mile climb to the Island in the Sky road with an elevation gain of 1,400 feet), and watched the moon set behind the monstrous Wingate wall to the west. At meeting the communal beer-and-tequila quota, though, I've been nothing but a slacker.

Sunni's disposition still matches her name: "Bagels, bacon, and hash browns— how does that sound, everybody?"

It sounds damn fine to me, and it tastes even better. We'll be burning a good 5,000 calories today, so desert indulgences such as bagel halves fried in bacon grease—a Chip Davis concoction "guaranteed to put my cardiologist in a new sailboat"—can legitimately be classified as cycling fuel.

There's plenty to occupy the grasshoppers while the ants pack up camp. Johno and I play some White Rim Frisbee without losing a single disc into the yawning maw of Gooseberry Canyon. Matt, checking the map, reports that today's ride (18.4 miles) will be only half as long as yesterday's (38.4 miles).

Chip: "That means we'll get to the campsite even later than we did last night, right?"

The scenery coaxes us off our bikes at the head of Monument Basin, where we clack carefully across the ripple rock for an unobstructed view of Canyonlands' best-known rock pillar—the distant and isolated 305-foot Totem Pole. Johno, ever on the edge, peers over the side and says, "Man, you'd be *luggage* if you fell off this!"

To find out just how mashed that baggage would be, we drop rocks over the side and clock their journey to the canyon floor. I count 6 seconds for a thrown rock and 4.6 seconds for a dropped one (your results may vary). Applying high-school physics for the acceleration of a falling body ($y = -\frac{1}{2} g t^2$), I calculate that we are standing 338.6 feet above the nearest landing place.

Before you brand such behavior Topographic Vandalism, may I remind you that a certain National Park Service employee heartily endorsed it? "To convince myself of the reality of change and therefore time," Ranger Abbey wrote in *Desert Solitaire*, "I will sometimes push a stone over the edge of a cliff and watch it descend and wait—lighting my pipe—for the report of its impact and disintegration to return." Abbey defended the practice as "aiding natural processes and verifying the hypotheses of geological morphology."

We turn onto a 1.5-mile spur to the White Crack Campsite, the nearest the White Rim Trail comes to the confluence of the Green and Colorado Rivers. It's an awesome run for me. Pedaling hard and gasping in the thin air, bunny-hopping trail rocks and riding confidently through deep sand for the first time, I arrive before any of the others on the barren, sunbaked rock shelf that many crystal gazers consider a supreme power spot—a geographic locus reputed to emanate psychic energy.

"What should we do for lunch?" asks Matt.

"How about lie in the shade and pant like dogs?" Chip replies.

So that's what we do. We drape a tarp from the truck to create a *ramada*—an open-air sun shelter—with a view of the La Sal Mountains to the east, the Abajos far to the south, and the red-and-white-banded rock spires of the park's Needles District closer at hand. In the jumbled wilderness of stone to the west stand

ABOVE / **Riders endure the death-march ascent of sandy Lathrop Canyon.** RIGHT / **Late-evening sunlight clarifies and colorizes rock strata in the sandstone walls atop the Shafer switchbacks.**

such lithic landmarks as the Dollhouse in the Maze District, then Lizard Rock, Chimney Rock, and 6,552-foot-high Elaterite Butte farther north.

Slugging water and wolfing classic biking grub—Cheddar cheese, hard salami, apples, cookies, granola bars— we watch a rainstorm approach. It brandishes virga, thunder, and lightning, but in our enervated states we hardly notice. Instead, we crawl into whatever patch of

shade we can find—under the ramada, beneath the truck, behind a pinyon pine—and test the suitability of this power spot for power naps.

Restored by siestas, we log a fast four miles to reach aptly named Vertigo Void. Here the White Rim sandstone reaches its maximum thickness visible from the trail—250 feet. "The thicker

this deposit," Todd Campbell explains in *Above and Beyond Slickrock,* "the more sheerly it tends to cleave off when undermined." Thus the "negative slope" of this site, where the painted cliff walls retreat so precipitously from the overhanging lip that everyone—even Johno—slithers on their bellies to the edge for a view. Gazing down on the ten-ton sandstone blocks that litter the canyon floor, we contemplate the cataclysmic concussions that must have occurred when they cracked off the White Rim and crashed hundreds of feet to their resting places below.

Cliff swallows work the canyon rim at 100 miles per hour with scarcely a wing flap, filling our frame of view like

EXOTIC INVADERS

Intruder alert: Tamarisk trees exert their steady chokehold on the Goose Neck of the Colorado River.

THE BRIGHTEST SPLASH OF GREEN IN THE DESERT IS NOT A DISPLAY OF LOCAL COLOR. It comes from tamarisk trees, a feathery-looking but tenacious species introduced to the United States from Eurasia in the early 1800s that now infests some river bottoms along the Green and Colorado waterways. A mature tamarisk tree can produce more than one million seeds per year and survive immersion for 70 days; it also tolerates drought and salty soil.

National-park managers have employed various remedies to stamp out tamarisk—chiefly cutting it back and burning it out—but the only thing likely to faze it would be the return of periodic flooding; before dams were built to control water flow, seasonal freshets scoured the river banks and channels. If these timely torrents were to be reinstated, they would very likely uproot the tamarisk trees, allowing native plants to reestablish themselves.

Ultimately, this "invasive exotic" (as scientists label harmful non-native species) may meet a homegrown nemesis: The coyote willow, writes natural historian Robert Webb in *Grand Canyon: A Century of Change,* "is shade tolerant and can become established under mature tamarisk trees. As old tamarisk trees die, they may be replaced by this native willow."

In the meantime, tamarisk will continue to flourish in the Western wilderness, threatening not just the overall ecological balance but also individual species. The endangered willow flycatcher, for example, has no choice but to nest in the impenetrable understory of the alien trees. Regrettably, says integrative biologist Tom Dudley, the flycatchers have fewer young than those nesting in native vegetation "because of fewer food resources associated with the exotics." One solution might be called rebugging: Biologists have introduced a leaf-feeding beetle from Kazakhstan that may soon help curtail the risk of tamarisk.

fighter planes in combat footage as they fly directly at us. Katie notes their chevron profiles: "Those things have rad-shaped wings."

"Check out my boat," calls Johno. He has crafted a "Utah boomerang"—bunchgrass blades tied together in just enough bulk that they hover in midair (and even return to their sender) when tossed over a precipice. Inspired by his example, I fold a guidebook page into a paper helicopter known as a whirligig, then launch it into the updraft. The whirligig spins serenely in space, barely deviating from its hover point some 15 feet above and beyond the cliff ledge.

Determined to pitch camp by daylight for a change, we press on. This southwestern segment of the trail commands a wide-open expanse of desert—one that allows riders to scout out the territory ahead. "Oh my God," Elizabeth suddenly exclaims, "look where the road goes!" She's gotten a glimpse of the brutal climb known as Murphy Hogback, with its 24 percent grade. Soon we're toiling up the hogback's quarter-mile-long, 320-foot-high ascent, floundering in crucibles that defy our lowest gears and highest efforts.

When the incline grows steep enough to defy the laws of physics, Elizabeth dismounts with aplomb, not disgust. "My strategy is to ride 'til I fall off the bike," she explains. "Then I get to walk!" Soon I'm out of my saddle—and pedals, too. If pushing the bike uphill generates a sweatbath this extreme, what

must it be like to ride the damn thing?

A black bird waddles into view at the top of the climb: "Hey, is that a raven up there?"

"No, it's a vulture," Elizabeth responds. "It's waiting for me to lie down!"

The brothers McBride continue their annoying habit of casually awaiting (and observing) our arrival atop the wickedest hills. Pete asks Chip, "How you feeling, big dog?"

"Great, but I think I left my lungs down there!"

Katie, uncharacteristically, is the last one up. Like spectators at the Salt Lake City Winter Olympics where Katie competed in 2002, we all scramble onto boulders at the top and cheer her ascent. Stoked by her fans (and, perhaps, by the novelty of *up*hill racing), Katie churns all the way up Murphy Hogback without a pause—then superhumanly repeats the feat three times for ski training.

The day's grind yields instant gratification: Murphy A, the loftiest and loveliest campsite we'll enjoy the entire trip, lies 200 yards beyond the top of the climb. Each person takes a turn in the changing room—the far side of the truck—and emerges in camp togs, ready for a beer and a clifftop view of the sunset.

The campsite threatens to make me a power-spot apostle. A perfectly flat council rock—head high and large enough to accommodate the eight of us sitting knee to knee—perches at the height of land, commanding a 360-degree view that fills those who behold it with the certainty

they are standing at the pinnacle of Creation. To the east rises a solid rock wall with a bite taken out; if there's any justice in this world, the moon will rise to fill it. To the south, the desert floor occasionally

Atop the "council rock" at Campsite A of Murphy Hogback, Elizabeth Hightower savors a storm-born breeze as Johno McBride contemplates the void.

gathers itself into the hulking table mountains of 5,464-foot Petes Mesa and its even taller cousin, 6,226-foot-high Ekker Butte. Away to the west stretches a land of spires and abysses that includes the Land of Standing Rocks, 11 miles across the Green River in the Maze District.

The elements vie for majesty with the landscape. Into the sky swirl simultaneous

Sunni, predicting bestsellerdom for *Sunni's Camp Cooking,* is acclaimed "the Martha Stewart of the Desert." It's an unfair comparison. Does anyone really believe the Doyenne of Domesticity could log the miles we did today, then turn out burritos as savory as these?

We've cycled together long enough now—three days—that this evening's lantern-light confidences devolve into hilarious rounds of "All-Time Most Embarrassing Moment." Sunni confesses that she once parachuted naked onto the 13th green of a golf course.

"Why'd you do that?" says Chip.

"Because it's traditional to skydive nude on your 200th jump!"

I know just how she felt. I go to sleep convinced that I've parachuted into the desert to star in "The Extreme Team Meets the Nutty Professor."

ANSWERING the desert's siren call at 3 a.m., I discover a nighttime fastness of gray rocks and silvered clouds, the antithesis of a rich sensory experience; the primary sensations are of quiet, of stillness, of a watchful waiting that stretches to eternity. Orion, which does not rise until after midnight in September, has become my familiar companion on these predawn peregrinations. I'm relieved to note I haven't started talking to the Hunter just yet.

Sleep finally comes an hour before a ground squirrel sounds my wake-up

apparitions of broody black storm clouds, hanging veils of backlit virga, distant jags of lightning, and rainbows anchored to the horizon in arcs or floating midair in patches. The only discordant note will sound much later on: The moon misses the cleft provided for it, then skitters behind a flock of clouds, threatening to grant us some unaccustomed sleep.

call: "Whasssup?" it screams in my ear, then flashes the white of its tail and scurries under a boulder. Two ravens swoop low and susurrant over the unmoving forms in camp, gulping their weird, six-note cry.

The desert tries on and discards new color schemes by the minute. Not a cyclist is stirring, so I decide to take off on a fast solo ride to the Candlestick campsite, ten miles distant. In the process I heedlessly blow right past a view of the Buttes of the Cross, named by Powell and his men. Then I lose the White Rim Trail—the price of following tire tracks in the dust—and head up the Soda Springs drainage, a dry wash filled with deep sand. It spills me onto some exposed rock, wounding my pride deeper than my knee.

I retrace my tracks to regain the trail. Like Butch Cassidy before me—his Robbers Roost gang is thought to have operated north of here in the 1880s—I'm still ahead of the posse. I stop to review my progress. There's a first far-away glimpse of the Green River channel, where vibrant green tamarisk trees choke the river bottom.

"How 'bout a refill?"

It's the voice of park ranger Paul Downey, welcoming me with an offer of water to the Candlestick campsite—a sun-blasted desolation near the base of stone-skirted Candlestick Tower. The fit-looking Downey, on a five-day backcountry tour, gladly takes time out from restocking the camp latrine with toilet paper to answer an Easterner's questions:

"It's been in the high 90s all week," says Downey, topping up my water bottles from a jerrican in the bed of his pickup. "Those bushes covered with yellow flowers can be rabbitbrush or broom snakeweed—they're often mistaken for each other."

When I mention *Desert Solitaire,* Downey—a veteran cyclist and river runner who has rafted the Colorado River's Cataract Canyon ten times—nods his head. "The spirit of Edward Abbey definitely still lives on down here in a big way."

I bring up the book's most notorious tale, in which the 11-year-old son of a murdered uranium prospector came close to surviving a 16-day desert ordeal that included a cliff plunge, a flash flood, and an unwitting psychedelic episode brought on by eating datura. Downey confirms that "datura is the hallucinogenic plant that grows in the mouths of canyons near rivers and streams. Some people eat it on purpose, but it's incredibly poisonous. We've never had a datura fatality in Canyonlands, but there was a nonfatal medical emergency in the Needles District several years ago.

"People who ingest the stuff get unbearably hot. Then, trying to cool down, they sometimes take off their clothes, increasing their exposure to the sun. Emergency-room workers are trained to look for three symptoms of datura consumption: red as a beet, hot as a hare, mad as a hatter."

I interrupt Downey as a cascading trill wafts up from the canyon nearby. "What's that—a cliff swallow?"

"No, that's a canyon wren," he says, deftly whistling its song. "The descending scale makes it easy to identify." I'm starting to think Downey could imitate its flight pattern too.

Downey tells me those Lathrop Canyon jet skiers had no business being there. "Jet skis have been banned in the park since 1997. When the ban first took effect, a bunch of jet skiers threatened to ride down the Green River and then up the Colorado. We let them know we'd have 14 rangers waiting for them, ready to take enforcement action. They decided not to make the ride."

Not that Downey's watch is uneventful. "We've had injuries from cyclists wiping out in the sand on the other side of Hardscrabble Hill—somebody broke a tandem frame in half there not too long ago. Another woman rolled a vehicle while trying to get it up Murphy Hogback. Vehicle tows out here cost $500 to $1,000; you're not allowed to abandon your car in the park even if the tow costs more than the vehicle."

The posse overtakes me and we pedal two short but brutally exposed miles to the intersecting Wilhite Trail. On our right, the hiking path snakes up through a narrow canyon, Holeman Spring Basin, on a five-mile jaunt to the Island in the Sky mesa top some 1,600 feet above. On

Bathed in moonlight that seems to rival the sun's illumination, Elizabeth Hightower does the "desert luge" on a sleep-defying pitch of the Shafer camp.

Cyclists stand silhouetted against tiers of Colorado Plateau sandstone stretching toward Mount Peale, the 12,721-foot apex of the distant La Sals.

our left, it vanishes into a deep, narrow, rock-walled gash in the desert floor; this is the start of the pinchy Holeman Slot Canyon, a sidewinding intestine of rock down which we propose to scramble.

As we swap our bike shoes for sandals, a few earlier arrivals clamber up out of the slot canyon. They are covered with mud and filled with bravado: "It's not too bad if you have a rope," they assure us. "It's no big deal if you know how to boulder."

We don't have a rope.

I don't know how to boulder.

the slot canyon wraps us in its cool, shadowy embrace.

The going is easy at first. But then comes a rock ledge protruding three feet from the canyon wall, offering a choice: Do you free-climb down the underhang or free-fall 12 feet or so into the pool of dirty brown water below it? Sunni volunteers to go first—a good thing, since she's the best climber in the group—and her descent is uneventful. Pete scrambles halfway down before falling backward into the quagmire.

This is just the recce Chip has been waiting for. He makes a heart-stopping leap straight into the center of the murk and comes up shaking his mane like a wet dog, sputtering muddy water as the huzzahs rain down: "Go Mud Man!" "Yo, Cave Creature!"

"You look like you fell in a vat of chocolate milk," Elizabeth informs him.

And me? Protesting that I'm perfectly happy to explore no farther, I am unceremoniously lowered into the muddy pool—and to each new canyon level beneath it—like a side of beef.

At the bottom of Holeman Slot Canyon is a smooth rock chute leading to a final muddy pool or—if you overshoot that—the lip of a 180-foot-high spillover and thence oblivion. Though awed by the payoff view (a box canyon so remote it has yet to be named), I'm just as happy to start climbing back toward the top: The pool at the bottom is emitting eerie bubbles, a sure sign that it harbors a sucking vortex or a stone Grendel.

And so, of course, we disappear at once into the Earth.

The shift from the sunbaked agoraphobia of the open desert to the close-in contours of these pulled-taffy walls is instantaneous and heaven-sent. We enter a realm of reflected golden light: Aqueous, radiant, tangible, it caroms down from a strip of blue high overhead as

Back in sunlight, we inventory the water supply. Only seven gallons remain. Though we are pedaling alongside the Green River, we can't drink from it without first filtering the water, boiling it, or treating it with iodine tablets. As a result, Elizabeth is overcome by waterlust: "Is that a mirage?" She thinks she's spotted a jerrican standing in the dusty dual tracks ahead, and—well, she has! We greedily fall upon this "gift from the water gods," as Katie puts it, filling our parched throats and bottles with its precious water and proving Abbey right: "A great thirst is a great joy when quenched in time."

Only when we've drunk our fill do we speculate how our salvation got here. Three possibilities: It fell overboard from a support vehicle; it was cached nearby, then discovered and left in mid-trail; or it was placed here on purpose by Rim Tours, whose name and 800 number are stenciled on the side of the container. If the third scenario is correct, it's the best bit of targeted marketing I've ever seen.

The refill makes it possible to vanquish Hardscrabble Hill, so wickedly steep that Katie climbs it just twice. Awaiting me at the top is a collared lizard—a common Canyonlands critter that can pull a reptilian wheelie and run on its hind legs for extra speed. I never see it leave all fours.

The Hardscrabble descent is harrowing in the extreme. Low rock overhangs crowd the trail from above. Treacherous drop-offs loom below it. With your eyes glued on those, your front wheel is apt to plunge into a lurking pocket of extra-

deep sand, pitching your bike into a handstand (panicky braking helps achieve this) and threatening to hurl you over the handlebars. Somehow I bring the rear wheel back to Earth, concluding that one needn't consummate an endo to experience its adrenaline rush.

Our final campsite, Labyrinth B, perches on a promontory boasting the delightful desert anomaly of a river view. The elements bestow some homecoming gifts: rain that actually reaches the ground (and blessedly us), then a rainbow, and finally a double rainbow.

I know just how the Kids are going to celebrate this harmonic convergence, and for once I beat them to the paunch: I throw off my clothes and stride down to the Green River for some ritualized skinny-dipping. The others dive right in—to the mud, that is. They roll in it, they writhe and wrestle in it, they slather it on their bodies and root about in it like giddy pigs. When I spy meticulous Matt using the gooey ooze to style his hair, I realize we're just one step removed from *Lord of the Flies.*

Honoring local tribal practices, Pete has shed his clothes, and now—as he points his camera at a clutch of revelers he's rounded up on the riverbank—it's a snap to supply the headline: "National Geographic Photographer Captures Prehistoric Mudpeople."

On this final night, after polishing off plates heaped with spaghetti and sausage accompanied by *salade en plastique*—fresh mesclun greens dressed with a

Dijon vinaigrette and presented in a Hefty sack—there will be no denying Morpheus. By the time the moon washes the gleaming constellations of Scorpio and Sagittarius from the sky around 10 p.m., we are all sound asleep.

I CELEBRATE a novel sensation—sleeping through the night—with a dawn dip in the river. I must be getting the hang of this wild life, because I climb from the water without taking most of the mud with me. Sunni orchestrates a positively sclerotic breakfast (pork chops, sausages, cheese-garlic grits). A final game of Ultimate Frisbee ensues. I sit on the bluff and admire the rock-spire parapets of this Paleozoic coliseum.

The short day—just 20 miles—contains only one climb, but it's a Sisyphean brute: The Mineral Bottom Road, once called Horsethief Trail, coils 1.5 miles of switchbacks into a 1,600-foot White Rim finale. (The agony of the ascent will become an ecstasy of triumph when I reach the top without dismounting.)

Riding side by side, Elizabeth and I marvel at three auto carcasses clinging to the switchbacks. They are riprap, a spectacularly innovative erosion-control measure. To me, however, they embody the Chip Davis outlook on life:

"Dude, how do you know where the edge is if you never cross it?"

Sky, rock, steel: Two-wheelers seem to find sanctuary beneath a desert rainbow. The surrounding flora is *Halogeton,* an exotic succulent.

Johno McBride negotiates the rock chute at the conclusion of Holeman Slot Canyon. At bottom lurks the murky pool and a stone shelf with a bird's-eye view of oblivion.

While exploring 59 miles of the Youghiogheny River, which flows from the Allegheny Mountains in West Virginia to the Monongahela River in Pennsylvania, two paddlers enjoy a quiet stretch just below Ohiopyle, Pennsylvania.

RIVER

CHAPTER FOUR

WILD

BY JOHN LANE / PHOTOGRAPHS BY SKIP BROWN

FROM MY kayak, I could hear the waterfall ahead. Our river guide, Chuck Stump, had told us about a boy who fell over the eight-foot drop after he lost his footing on shore. His parents watched in horror, searching for him everywhere, but he never resurfaced. Eighteen hours later, while the parents were treated for shock in a local hospital, divers found the child shivering, but safe, on a rock shelf behind the waterfall. The boy had sat there for almost a day staring through the falling water, without being able to get out—the same falling water I was hearing now and was about to drop over in my boat.

I looked at my paddling partner, Watts Hudgens, a younger colleague at the college where I teach in South Carolina. With it being June and the term over, we jumped at the chance to head for the mountains of West Virginia, Maryland, and Pennsylvania to kayak the Youghiogheny River from near its headwaters on down. It was a river adventure we wanted, an old tradition. Henry David Thoreau, the famous nature writer who lived from 1817-1862, and his brother had spent a week paddling the placid waters of New England's Concord and Merrimack Rivers. The 19th-century pioneer John Wesley Powell explored the Colorado and the Green through the Grand Canyon between 1869 and 1875.

LEFT / **Two kayakers sneak down the left side of 16-foot Swallow Falls, the first major rapid on the upper reaches of the Youghiogheny River in Maryland.** ABOVE / **Four local girls from Friendsville swim in the Youghiogheny River.**

I didn't think our journey would end up as exciting as John Wesley Powell's, with capsized boats, sudden storms, and depleted rations, but I have to admit that up front I had some fears.

I'd been kayaking for 20 years, so you couldn't say I was afraid of paddling rivers. It was this particular river that frightened me. The Youghiogheny's whitewater is legendary, and it had been years since I'd really pushed my rusty kayaking skills. I'd researched the river's rapids and talked to friends who knew the river—they assured me my caution was well-founded. There was no way around it: I was a middle-aged paddler facing some furious water on the Youghiogheny.

Guidebooks, which I had read as if they contained sacred text, pointed out that on this first six-mile section, called the Top Yough, there were three tricky rapids— Swallow Falls, Swallowtail Falls, and the ominous Suckhole. We now sat at the top of the second of them. Minutes before, Chuck had successfully run 16-foot Swallow Falls, and Watts and I had cautiously exited our boats and walked around it, short-circuiting our adventure temporarily. The walk was easy because it was along a popular trail in the surrounding state park.

Now I faced Swallowtail Falls, about half the size of its bypassed sister back upstream. I looked onshore for another place to land my boat and walk around the rapid. Chuck saw my reluctance and assured me it was a simple run. It was time to commit to the adventure. Following closely behind Chuck, I dug my paddle in just as he did, following his every move. I could see where I needed the boat to go, but it seemed the water conspired against me, pushing the boat in all the wrong places.

Finally, heart pounding, I paddled two strokes and fell like a leaf over the lip of the falls. I felt the river drop away as if the water was going down a drain. Then, I was sitting safely in the calm eddy water below. I had made it, as did Watts—we had avoided the fate of the little boy.

I looked back upstream at the river as it poured over the sandstone rock that created the drop. In the next five days, like the water, we would head downstream, covering 59 miles of whitewater on this legendary East Coast river as it flowed from near its birthplace in the Allegheny Mountains to its end in southwestern Pennsylvania, where it then calmly empties into the Monongahela.

Our kayaking adventure on the Youghiogheny was underway.

THE YOUGHIOGHENY,

or "Yough" as the locals call it, the Tygart Valley River, and the Cheat River flow into the Monongahela, which drains into the Ohio, and ultimately the Mississippi River. The Yough's headwaters form among bold springs and fern-studded seeps on the western slope of Backbone Mountain just above Silver Lake, which is a few hundred yards into West Virginia.

The river here is small enough to step across. Below Silver Lake, the Yough meanders through alder and maple thickets, working its way into Maryland. Native trout thrive as do beaver. Tidy farms line the banks within the first 30 miles as the river keeps to the fertile valley between Backbone Mountain and Chestnut Ridge.

As the Youghiogheny gains water and gradient, whitewater rapids come to life. Rafters and kayakers have labeled certain parts of the 150-mile river that have particularly good rapids, giving each section a name that correlates to its proximity to the headwaters. Closest is called the Tippy Top Yough; it is followed by the Top, and then the legendary Upper. The

Middle, a fast, isolated section of the river, comes next. The Lower, which begins in Ohiopyle, Pennsylvania, is one of the most rafted sections of river on the East Coast. The Bottom Yough, perhaps the most beautiful of the river's reaches, offers broad sky vistas and encompasses a wide expanse of water with long cobble shoals and the occasional rapid as the river carves through Chestnut Ridge. Finally, the river joins with the Monongahela, named for the Native Americans who lived there around 1600.

After Chuck, Watts, and I ran

Hungry after paddling, Steve Strothers pulls his boat toward a store in Friendsville, Maryland, which sells food and drinks.

Swallowtail Falls, I relaxed. To the left, Muddy Creek toppled over a 54-foot, breathtaking drop. I enjoyed the way the Yough heaved and gurgled through the house-size boulders clogging the river-bed. It was like a bumper-car ride, except you did not want to hit the objects in your path. I watched Chuck, who knew this run intimately, pull his boat through slots between the rocks.

What was the worst thing that could happen to me? Death? Not likely. Injury? Maybe, but I knew I had a long history of paddling behind me to draw upon. I followed without incident through rapids called Best Boof and Better Boof. We worked our way toward Suckhole, my next challenge.

had gargled and swallowed more than a few paddlers. All had passed through the hole in the rocks where it seemed half the river was headed before it disappeared; Suckhole had spit them out. Chuck saw no reason to believe that if worse came to worst, things wouldn't be any different for us. I could feel Suckhole pulling at me like a magnet.

I didn't like the looks of things—call it an intuition, something important for a middle-aged paddler. I told Chuck I planned to walk this one. He shook his head, but accepted my decision. I paddled my boat over to the bank, shouldered it, and walked an old railroad embankment to the bottom of the powerful rapid. Safely back in my boat, I watched as Chuck and Watts tumbled through the shoot to the right of the infamous hydraulic.

"Good call," Watts said as he slipped into the eddy next to me. "That was the hardest rapid yet."

THE HUMAN history of the Yough is as complex as one of the Top Yough's rapids. Paleo-Indians arrived around 8000 B.C. By A.D. 1600, they lived within the watershed. No one really knows when or why they disappeared, but they left their name for the Monongahela River that

Approaching Suckhole, my panic returned. I followed Chuck into a small eddy and looked downstream. He pointed with his paddle at a snarl of sticks on the right side of the river and at a bubbling eddy right in front of it. "That's Suckhole," he said. I knew from the accounts in the river guidebooks that this rapid and its infamous suckhole

Kayaker Dale Herring surfs a glassy wave on the Upper Yough. Whitewater features like waves and holes allow kayaking enthusiasts to think of rivers as natural amusement parks.

An aerial view of the Youghiogheny reveals a straight, silvery stretch of river contrasted by the dark reaches of the Allegheny Mountains.

joins the Yough at McKeesport, just downstream from Pittsburgh. By 1737 the Youghiogheny River began to appear on maps.

George Washington first journeyed into the headwaters of the Yough in 1753. Washington believed controlling the Youghiogheny was key to curtailing the French's access to the drainage. Yet, during the opening battle of the French and Indian Wars in 1754, 22-year-old Col. Washington and his detachment of troops that he commanded were defeated in that area, at Fort Necessity in the Great Meadow (11 miles east of present-day Uniontown).

After the war, settlers followed Washington's westward trail and remained in valleys such as those found where Sang Run Bridge crosses the Youghiogheny. "Sang," or ginseng, a wild plant with a curative root, is said to have been common in the area. For the old-timers, hunting sang provided a steady source of cash. Today, whitewater outfitters have provided a new kind of gold for the hills of western Maryland.

We finished the Top Yough, but I worried about the Upper—eight miles of rapids known around the world as proving grounds for the best paddlers. As we loaded our boats and drove back to the motel, I thought about the stories I'd heard about the Upper Yough's continuous rapids. I wondered if I was prepared for such a difficult day of paddling. The Top Yough had been a good warm-up with stretches of whitewater punctuated with difficult rapids (two of which I had walked), but it would be nothing like the Upper Yough.

Ed Gertler, author of *Maryland and Deleware Canoe Trails*, called the Upper Yough "the big whitewater challenge...unrelenting boulder piles, blocked views, unobvious passages, menacing undercuts and technical difficulties." A recent account of the passage in *Appalachian Whitewater: The Northern States,* edited by John Connelly and others, calls it "the ultimate whitewater run for expert paddlers in Maryland. It is one of the premier streams in the entire eastern United States."

We would be in good hands, though. I had arranged for two guides, Steve Strothers and Terry Peterson, to lead us on our second day of paddling. We were to meet them at 11 a.m. in front of Mountain Surf, a whitewater apparel manufacturer in Friendsville, Maryland.

The scene in Friendsville was youthful and electric. Boaters who could just as easily be surfers or skateboarders hung out in front of Mountain Surf waiting for friends. Everyone had a nickname. The chatter was relentlessly aquatic.

Our guides arrived. Steve works as a cartographer for the U.S. National Imagery and Mapping Agency in Washington, D.C., but spends weekends paddling the river three hours west of the capital. Terry was a raft guide for 15 years, but now kayaks for fun while she works as a graduate-school teacher.

We all drove to the boat launch that

has a gravel parking lot along the river. It is known as the Sang Run put-in. The Yough looked surprisingly serene as it passed by. I slipped on my gear as I listened to Terry and Steve discuss the complex politics of the river and how establishing a parking area was no small feat. Access to the river has always been contested, and only in the last ten years—when a river conservation group, American Whitewater, fought for the establishment of a Maryland Department of Natural Resources parking lot—had it become easy to leave a car at the put-in. The conservationists also worked with the operators of the upstream dam at Deep Creek Lake to have regular releases of water so raft companies and kayakers could plan trips.

Local residents used to make recreational boating difficult, sometimes even firing a rifle at whitewater enthusiasts. Rafters would stop on the bridge, throw their rubber craft in the river, and climb down the bridge abutment as a friend drove the car away.

After we geared up—neoprene skirts that keep water out of the kayak, life vests for flotation, helmets to keep our heads safe, and splash jackets for warmth— Steve looked at the river and announced,

Rafters decked out in yellow helmets and life jackets listen to a guide give safety instructions prior to braving the Class III-IV whitewater of the Lower Yough.

"That's about as good as it's going to get."

I slipped into the current. The water was flat but moving fast—it gave me time to think about what was below. I knew I would be challenged to the edge of my abilities. I was excited about that, but also nervous. I felt that deep emptiness in my stomach that comes from fear—from anticipation of the unknown. My arms felt weak as I pulled myself downstream with the current. I knew that I would drop with the wild river more than 600 feet through one of the most rugged gorges in the East before I stepped out of my boat later in

Kayakers such as Mike Nosal (front) run the chaotic water that makes up the renowned rapids of the Upper Yough.

the day in Friendsville—what a comforting name for a take-out on one of the toughest whitewater runs around!

A few miles later, after passing Sang Run Bridge, the Upper Yough takes on the characteristics Ed Gertler had described—narrow, continuous, technical. I knew that in an hour or so I would approach the rapids I'd read about in the guidebooks. "Exercise good judgment regarding your boating skills," one river guide urged, and have "expertise, bravado, and life insurance."

One person, a rafter, has died on the Upper Yough. I didn't plan to be the second person. I believe the low statistic to be a credit to the overall experience of boaters on this run. Everyone tends not only to be friends, but also to watch each other's back. Since the river is so difficult, just to get on it usually takes some kind of mentor who feels that you are ready to take it on if guided down.

I followed Steve for a couple more miles before going through what many call the gateway to the river, a sloping drop called Gap Falls. Below that is continuous "boogie water," or rapid, but playful, currents. It wasn't that scary, just pure fun—waves shattering on the boat, small ledges breaking the river into small washboards, backwashes, and eddies. Then things became more difficult.

My stomach began to tighten. I stopped to eat two granola bars before continuing. It helped a little and gave me energy for the next three-to-four miles of adventure I was waiting for. The steep, narrow rapids drop 100 feet over the next mile, starting with Bastard, Charlie's Choice, Triple Drop, and finally National Falls. It is known as the Miracle Mile, but it blurred together in my mind as I followed Steve and Terry through constricted channel after constricted channel. At the bottom of Triple Drop I found myself buried up to my shoulders in a foaming hydraulic. I reached with my paddle for the calmer water in an eddy behind a nearby, 12-foot rock. There, Steve sat in his kayak calmly. He smiled, knowing that I was experiencing the beauty and power of the Upper Yough.

Sitting in the eddy was no comfort, though. As far as I could see, there was no getting out of the Yough's gorge except by water—or a long walk to the distant top of the ridge. Though my heart was thumping, I was determined to work my way to the end of the run—still five miles downstream.

Several rapids later, I saw Steve's face get more serious. "This is one of the more dangerous rapids on the river," he said as we entered a Class IV-V rapid called Heinzerling. I followed Steve and Terry as they slipped through an impossibly narrow blind slot into a big eddy shaded with sycamores. "If you didn't know that slot was there, you'd head right into the worst of it," Steve said, relaxing in the eddy.

As I sat in the eddy, I looked over my shoulder and down came a boater in a five-meter racing kayak known as a wildwater boat. It looked almost impossible to manage because it was so long and light, but even more surprising was that the boater had no paddle, only little black flippers on his hands. He was smiling as he went straight through the passage Steve called "the rifle barrel."

"That's Jeff Snyder," Steve said.

I knew Jeff and his brother Jim were some of the pioneers of paddling. Steve did not seem surprised to see him in a boat without a paddle.

"Does he do that often?" I asked.

"Unprecedented," Steve smiled. "Probably the first person ever to have done it."

I looked back over my shoulder. Below the rifle barrel, Jeff had the

ABOVE / Two paddlers await a dam release that will send enough water down the Upper Yough for kayakers to paddle its rapids. RIGHT / Outfitters in Ohiopyle, Pennsylvania, offer mountain biking, rafting, canoeing, and kayaking.

wildwater boat standing on its end as it slammed into the water pillowing against the rock and then rode the current down to the left.

Steve followed Jeff's downstream. I watched his route, how he, too, rode up on the pillow that had stood Jeff's boat vertical, but that also allowed them to miss worse water to the left. I shook my head. "They're putting their boats on end on purpose," I muttered. I took several strokes and dropped into 20 yards of impossibly chaotic, slanted, exploding water, "the death slot" on the left, and the big pillow rock with a quarter of the river piling against it on the right. As I popped through the offset waves, all I could see was the

chaos below. I missed the pillow and somehow punched through the grabby hydraulics at the rapid's bottom.

IT WAS in Class IV-V Heinzerling that I saw most clearly how the dance of water and stone on a whitewater river speaks of challenge and risk. This slippery equation between the two is at the heart of adventure sports such as whitewater kayaking. When is a river too difficult? When is it best to stand on shore and admire a serious stretch of gradient? The lucky ones among us get to chase the answer to that question down a wild rapid like Heinzerling, and make it through.

Visitors enjoy the spring weather and good view at River's Edge, a bed-and-breakfast in the historic town of Confluence, Pennsylvania.

FALLINGWATER

Frank Lloyd Wright created Fallingwater above Bear Run, a tributary of the Youghiogheny River.

IN THE EARLY 1930s, WHEN FAMED AMERICAN ARCHITECT FRANK LLOYD WRIGHT FIRST visited Bear Run, a swift, rocky tributary of the Youghiogheny that ends near Ohiopyle, he stood on a boulder above the creek and imagined a house with "broad terraced levels picturesquely related to the water." Wright wanted to marry the building site to his architectural creation—a trademark of his original designs in both public and private buildings.

When Edgar J. Kaufmann, a department store heir from Pittsburgh, commissioned the architect to design his summer home, the creation of Fallingwater began. The boulder where Wright stood became the hearth, and Wright designed the house of horizontal layers mimicking the ledges of the local Pottsville sandstone. His bold design cantilevered the main floor out over the striking waterfall, and he even created a hatch in the open living room where it was possible to walk down a flight of steps and enter the stream.

Walking through the house, one hears birdsongs and water sounds melding as if walls and floors do not exist. On the edge of the living space, water seeps into a crevice and flows out of the house under a section of glass. Indirect lighting, a Wright staple, adds to the feeling of openness. The floor plan is accented in Fallingwater's bedrooms by "structural folds," a lowering of the ceiling as one goes deeper into each sleeping space, drawing the eye outside.

In 1963 the Kaufmann family entrusted Fallingwater to the Western Pennsylvania Conservancy, an organization dedicated to saving such significant places. The Western Pennsylvania Conservancy has expanded the Kaufmann's original 1,600 acres to 5,000, encompassing and protecting the entire headwaters of Bear Run. It is possible on the grounds to experience the beauty of the Youghiogheny watershed.

One mile downstream from the take-out for the Upper Yough, the wild river disappears into 16-mile-long Youghiogheny Lake, finished by the Corps of Engineers for flood control in 1943. The lake, the only major reservoir on the Youghiogheny, provides recreation of a different sort. On warm days, the whining of jet skis can be heard as they create wakes in the jade-green water.

After our successful run on the Upper Yough, we stayed just downstream from the Youghiogheny Lake dam at the River's Edge. The bed-and-breakfast in Confluence, Pennsylvania, caters to the tourists drawn to town by the river and the bike trail that runs from Pittsburgh to Cumberland. Just off the main street, the Casselman, the Yough's largest tributary, joins with the river and Laurel Hill Creek to form what Washington and the early explorers called the Turkey Foot.

Early the next morning Watts and I slipped down the bank amid a din of indignant geese. We found flat water, but knew that downstream were five or six good rapids, though nothing like those we had seen the day before on the Upper Yough. This would be a float trip more than a wild whitewater adventure. It would prove a time to slip downstream and think about rivers.

While floating down the Concord, Thoreau mused, "at last I resolved to launch myself on its bosom and float whither it would bear me." That's the heart and soul of adventure—to give yourself up to time, to experience, I thought as we began our own float toward Ohiopyle.

Along the left bank of this stretch, known as the Middle Yough, runs the backbone of a contemporary recreational industry: the bike path stretching more than 70 miles downstream. A hard-packed sandstone trail, the path is set on the bed of an abandoned railway that, in its heyday, made Washington's idea of a canal obsolete in less than 100 years.

As we floated past the Turkey Foot, I thought about Washington's first canoe trip downstream. Unlike us, the father of this country had big industry on his mind—a trade route via water to the Ohio River—and he probably never could have imagined such confluence of modern desires as we could see from the Middle Yough.

What became known as the Braddock Road, was improved, and rerouted to become, in 1806, the first federally funded highway. The Pennsylvania section was complete by 1818. This highway, known as the National Road, ran from Cumberland, Maryland, to Wheeling, Virginia (originally)—now West Virginia—and now runs all the way to San Francisco. The road crossed the Youghiogheny just above the site of today's town of Confluence, at an old ford called the Great Crossings. The bridge that was built for the National Road across the Yough is now below the waters of Lake Youghiogheny. Sometimes, if the water has been dropped far enough, you can

see the three-span stone bridge appear like a ghost from the nation's childhood just downstream of the present-day U.S. Route 40 crossing.

A shredder, which is a locally manufactured cataraft designed in 1986 by Tom Love, is the perfect boat for running easy rapids, fishing, or simply relaxing.

Downstream is gorge country, with sharp Pennsylvania ridges descending 1,000 feet to the river. If the Yough has a soul, it lingers in the broad peopleless floodplain within the horseshoe bend called Victoria Flats below Confluence, where the coal-mining town of Victoria once stood. We looked for the ruins of the town, but found nothing.

uncommon, this collision of train and deer. The bones of another deer—a young male with spikes for a rack—rested less than 20 yards up the tracks.

Soon we were back on the water. Halfway from Confluence to Ohiopyle we passed into Ohiopyle State Park, a 19,000-acre preserve. Within the state park's sanctuary, we drifted downstream. As we looked around contentedly, I went deep inside my thoughts to contemplate waves, trees, the shore, and the mountains beyond. The woods along the river are mostly second-growth, 30 or 40 years old, though Watts pointed out one huge hemlock in the woods that could have seen centuries of water passing downstream.

Five more miles of fast, flat water broken by occasional ripples and we could see the Ohiopyle railroad bridge ahead. We went to shore and got out of our kayaks because 18-foot Ohiopyle Falls was just below. We could see cables across the river to catch unaware boaters who might float down from the Middle Yough toward the falls.

We then followed a tiny trail inland through dense spring wildflowers that included many jack-in-the-pulpits growing under sycamore and river birch. We climbed the hill to a railroad and saw five vultures take to the air from the fresh carcass of a white-tailed deer killed by a train. As we walked the tracks, we noticed that this was not

THERE'S no place like Ohiopyle, no place that even comes close," Tim Palmer wrote in his epic 1980s narrative *Youghiogheny: Appalachian River.* "All roads out of Ohiopyle are climbed in second gear. All roads into Ohiopyle burn the brakes." After walking around the falls and entering the nearby town, we could see what Palmer meant. The green

slopes of the Yough's formidable gorge slipped down to the edge of the river on one side and on the other formed the backdrop for parking lots and a few old buildings. There stood the old general store, now Falls Market & Inn, several churches, a train station, and several dozen white clapboard houses.

Earlier in the week I had commented to Watts that the young Upper Yough boaters, with their trendy short boats, dreadlocks, and their ritual of hanging out at the wall in front of the Mountain

The Lower Yough provides a perfect introduction for kayakers and rafters to the skills and thrills of river-running. One hundred thousand people visit this part of the river each year.

Surf, made Friendsville seem like the grunge capital of kayaking.

"These are *my* people," I said, laughing and pointing at the cars parked in the private boaters' parking lot on the lower Yough. On the boat racks were ten-year-old kayaks, long Perception and Dagger boats in discontinued colors. The boaters mostly looked like middle-age professionals out to redline their excitement meters on a day off.

Ohiopyle has been a recreational bonanza, a rafting capital of the East, since the early 1960s. Because of the continuous releases of water from Lake Youghiogheny, the commercial rafting traffic can continue all summer when everything else in the mountains is dry.

The Corps of Engineers regulates its release of water, and the state of Pennsylvania regulates the paddling in Ohiopyle. Five rafting companies operate there, with 100,000 tourists a year parceled out among them, each company floating them down the seven miles of the exciting, though not usually pushy, Lower Yough.

It was easy to see that the anarchy and alchemy of Friendsville was far behind. The dam upstream of Confluence provides predictable daily flow all summer. On the Lower Yough the private boaters must compete for several thousand permits, and launch times are assigned according to availability. Even "the shuttle," the way paddlers set up cars so there is one at the beginning of the river and one at the end, is complex and bureaucratic, a sharp contrast to the recently settled boating frontier just 30 miles upstream on the Upper. Private boaters in Ohiopyle must purchase a token to ride a bus back from the take-out to their vehicles parked a mile or so up the hill from the river.

The next day we hooked up with Laurel Highlands River Tours for the 11 a.m. commercial trip down the Lower Yough. Here, the river drops 27 feet per mile from the bottom of the falls to Bruner Run take-out, seven miles downstream. There are 14 named rapids, many of them Class III, and some even Class IV at higher water levels. Many of the best drops are in the first mile of the river, and often kayakers will put in, and

run this section called The Loop because afterwards they can walk their boats across the peninsula and loop back to the parking lot.

When we arrived to paddle, the river was at a good level, almost three feet. The rain had helped bring the water level up. I asked the general manager of Laurel Highlands about our desire to paddle the last leg of the river, down to South Connellsville, and he said, "You've got to go down with Cube, a guide of ours who grew up on the river and fishes that stretch. I think he's got tomorrow off."

He pointed to the staging area for the rafts. Cube was pumping up a raft. He had long gray hair pulled in a ponytail under his "Lawyers.com" cap. Cube agreed to meet us the next morning; he said that he would paddle down with us in his shredder, an inflatable catamaran, a popular craft of local design paddled often on the Upper and Lower Yough.

"What can I expect of that final stretch?" I asked Cube. "You're gonna love it," he said. "No access except by river. It's bear and train country."

The next day, our final on the river, was shaping up to be another adventure, with Cube as our guide. But first, the famous Lower Yough still awaited us. The Laurel Ridge trip had three rafts with 15 brave adventurers. These guests were mostly British, from the Royal Air Force. "They come over every year," Bo Harshyne, the trip leader explained. "We had a group of pilots come over one year, you know, the kind that can do face plants on mountain bikes and get back up and keep going. You couldn't stop those guys." During the July-August high season, the outfitter might have 80 people on a trip.

We put in with the commercial trip in the pool below Ohiopyle Falls. There's a big bubble of water at the falls' base and we worked against the strong current to paddle up on it, but the current pushed us downstream. I thought about how every October many local boaters run these falls on Falls Race Day.

Chuck Stump, our guide on the Top Yough, had said that this past year he ran it nine times in one day and he couldn't understand why it wasn't open for business all year. "Over a thousand runs on the Falls Race Day and nothing bad happened. I saw Jeff Snyder go over it standing up in an inflatable kayak."

We followed Cube, who was charged with rescuing clients if they fell out of their raft, through Entrance Rapid. This rapid was the first of a series along The Loop—geographically, an oxbow where the Youghiogheny doubles back on itself. The peninsula in the middle, called Ferncliff, is a nature preserve and National Natural Landmark.

When we hit the second rapid, called Cucumber, one of the rafts flipped upside down. We could see yellow helmets and paddles bobbing in the froth ahead of us. The vacationing pilots were laughing as they swept past. The river looked like a floating yard sale. I was concerned for the bobbing bodies, but I finally laughed and commented to Watts that this was tilting the adventure meter for these tourists. Not nearly as difficult or exhausting as the Upper Yough, the Lower offers pure recreation. It felt good to be on the water, breaking through the three-foot waves and punching into eddies that moved like liquid conveyor belts.

Six miles after the loop, we slipped through standing waves and past big slabs of sandstone rocks. One rapid, a Class III-IV called Dimple Rapids, has claimed three lives in the last year. I sat in a downstream eddy impressed with the safety precautions Laurel Highlands River Tours took with their trip. The trip leader stood on top of the rock with a whistle, moving rafts like a traffic cop, but ready with rescue ropes if necessary. All the Laurel Highlands rafts made it through, the RAF airmen slapping paddles in the fast, constricted channel below the deadly undercut rock. Other outfitters were not so lucky. Five rental rafts with no guide—what the outfitters call "unguided missiles," flipped, some dangerously close to the rock. The rafters floated downstream, paralyzed in fear.

At first I watched as other kayakers rushed into the current and pulled the bobbing boaters ejected from the raft into the calmer side eddies. Some customers, with no kayak to rescue them, bobbed 50 yards downstream until they lodged like litter among boulders. Finally out of the current, they flopped like exhausted trout on the gravel.

Paddling out to do my part in the rescue, I took several strokes and entered the current, quickly snagging one of the helpless—a middle-age man like myself, out for a day's worth of adventure. I could see from the look on his face that he'd already filled his quota. He latched onto the back of my boat and I dragged him slowly toward calmer water, where he could finally stand up safely and wait to be retrieved by the crew now reassembling downstream.

IT WAS quite a show. In spite of Dimple Rapid and its deadly reputation, a hundred thousand people float the Lower Yough every year.

All the way to River's End, the last big Class III-IV rapid on the run before the take-out at Bruner's, I watched the faces of boaters—many had never before experienced whitewater. They appeared to be having a great time.

It was raining the next day when the Laurel Highlands truck dropped us off at the Bruner Run take-out, now our put-in for our final 10-mile float down the Bottom Yough to South Connellsville. This was where the Yough would leave the mountains behind. Just downstream from Bruner's, the high tourist energy of

Hemlock-lined banks frame 54-foot-high Muddy Creek Falls just before it flows into the Top Yough in Maryland.

the Lower section recedes into memory and river miles.

"If you focus on the right things," Rick Bass wrote in *Wild to the Heart*, you can find wildness and freedom anywhere, I am convinced." On our final day on the river I was focused on what Cube had called "the wildest, most beautiful section of the Yough."

I could see Cube was right from our first moment. The ridges on the Bottom Yough are high and green, constricting the river into a tight gorge. The water runs swift and pure. It was as if the

Paddlers stop in an eddy for a rest, or to wait their turn for a chance to surf a small wave on the Upper Yough in Maryland.

landscape, in its last 10 miles of mountain wildness, was intent on holding the river for itself. There were no rapids as long or difficult as we had seen upstream on the Top, the Upper, and the Lower, but there was something—call it isolation or distance—that made the Bottom Yough feel freer than any stretch above it.

We drifted downstream, Cube and Watts paddling a shredder, a type of black rubber catamaran the size of a commercial raft. I watched as they paddled out in front of me in a band of soft mist. Cube had his fishing rod with him and in a broad eddy he cast into the current. The river had always provided. "Once I was sitting in this eddy," Cube said. "It was midday and I was hungry.

The fish weren't biting." Upstream, floating down from the Lower Yough like a tiny raft, was a bright red box, bobbing in the wave train. Cube said the box floated into the calm water behind a rock where he was sitting. "It was a Tupperware container and inside was a full lunch just packed that morning," he explained, laughing.

By lunchtime, we had drifted through the last rapid before the industrial town of South Connellsville. We pulled our boats out on a cobble beach where the local teenagers had positioned slabs of river-worn sandstone to form a bench, a Fred Flintstone sofa.

Upstream we could see the Yough carving through the mountain gorge the tourists frequented. Downstream, Cube pointed out a boulder the locals call Turtle Rock. Generations of South Connellsville teenagers had painted the large boulder in a hundred different hues. It marked the head of a large island where Cube had once lived for more than a year.

Close by his boyhood home, Cube had built a lean-to out of pallets there, eaten fish from the river, and picked up firewood from the railroad right-of-way. "I was livin' like a Buddhist monk," Cube explained, staring downstream at the site of his own personal Walden. He left that paradise to work on the river as a guide, to show other people his home river.

A few miles downstream, the large industrial city of Connellsville diverts the river into a water filtration plant.

From Turtle Rock the Youghiogheny has 46 miles before it disappears into the Monongahela just south of Pittsburgh.

If the Youghiogheny has a wild heart, it pulses in the waterfalls, narrow rock jams, abundant forests, and turbulent whitewater all along its length. On my journey downriver, I found the heart of the river also beating strongly in Cube, and others like him. Before we hauled our boats across the railroad tracks to my truck, the three of us sat on the bench and looked out at the river. You could see that Cube loved every inch of the flowing water coming down all the way from West Virginia.

My Youghiogheny river adventure ended there on that cobble-strewn beach within sight of the river's last small rapid. Had it been worth it? On the trip up from South Carolina I had expressed doubt to Watts that a middle-age college professor should risk such difficult new whitewater. He reminded me how much I have always loved paddling and how seldom someone is given eight days on a wild river as various as the Youghiogheny. Watts was right. Adventure is only possible if you are willing to stretch a little.

Downstream, the river continued its slow journey toward the Gulf of Mexico. Upstream, the current worked its magic against stone, and paddlers entered the current for a day of challenge. I followed Cube's eyes as they took in the river and watched it pass on toward Pittsburgh.

John Lane (right) and Watts Hudgens paddle between major stretches of white-water near the middle of their 59-mile odyssey near Confluence, Pennsylvania.

Sunlight fades on the Cabrillo Highway, California 1, near Kirk Creek at Big Sur, California, during a three-week, father-and-son adventure up the West Coast of the United States.

COASTAL
CRUISING

CHAPTER FIVE

BY PATRICK J. KELLY / PHOTOGRAPHS BY MIGUEL LUIS FAIRBANKS

I HAVE NOT bathed, shaved, or slept in a bed in three days and I feel great. I am, after all, an adventurer astride a factory-fresh, metallic-silver, BMW R 1150 GS—the SUV of motorcycles. Imagine a 600-pound, dual-sport machine that can blow past anything on the interstate, hold her own in the corners, or rumble up a fire lane in the forest. *Liebchen,* (German for sweetheart), is loaded down like a rented mule—145 pounds of that load being my 16-year-old son, Eddie. He is napping against my shoulder as we carve our way north along the Cabrillo Highway near Big Sur, California. We'll continue to hug this road until we hit Washington's Olympic Peninsula, where our motorcycle rental insurance coverage stops. Along the way we'll camp, climb, cave, hike,

windsurf, and hang glide at sites on the West Coast. Ed is missing some dramatic scenery here near Big Sur—blue ocean and sparkling surf crashing against the rocky shoreline hundreds of feet below, a setting sun blasting everything with that special orange hue, and the pungent sea and forest wafting through my open-face shield.

We didn't start out as adventurers, but as tourists. We experienced the daily circus along a two-mile, paved strip at

LEFT / Author Pat Kelly and his son, Ed, fuel-up before continuing north on California 1 through the redwood forest near Big Sur, California. ABOVE / Photographer Miguel Fairbanks finds adventure along California 1 as he parachutes in tandem near Vandenberg Air Force Base with Skydive Santa Barbara owner, David Hughes.

Venice, California, where we had our names engraved on a grain of rice, consulted a psychic ("adventure awaits"), paid a buck to pose with an inflatable space-alien couple in beachwear, watched the muscle-heads pump iron while the bikinis skated by on inline skates. We bought fake tattoos and learned a new word—*Touron*, a hybrid of "tourist" and "moron."

Tourist time over—we cut inland to U.S. Route 101 north to begin a 300-mile jaunt to Pinnacles National Monument. Pinnacles is a popular destination in central California for rock climbers of all skill levels. We'll need to do some riding, though, to get there before dark. This will be our first night camping and I'd prefer to see what we packed without having to use flashlights.

By the time we reach Pinnacles National Monument, the sun is setting on a twisting, one-lane gravel road. We ride through a dwarf forest of blue oak sprinkled over rolling, grassy foothills and mini canyons—I think of African savannah. The Pinnacles themselves, formations of towering, pinkish rock that resemble impacted dragon teeth, are visible a mile or so away. This is when "the incident" occurs.

I can only imagine what the park ranger thinks—20 minutes left in his shift, when he hears the soft rumble of a thoroughbred motorcycle approaching and sees two riders in matching red-and-black adventure apparel. They putter sensibly around the steep, tight corner, stop to ask a question, then promptly roll over

into the ditch on the side of the road—*Crunch! Vrrrooomm!*

"She's not so new anymore," Eddie says, scrambling to his feet, looking at the fallen motorcycle.

"Lift!" I yell, straining at the handle-bars. "She's suffering!"

"Kill the motor," the ranger shouts, running over to help us.

NEVER RIDE FASTER
THAN YOUR ANGEL CAN FLY

HUMBOLDT COUNTY CA
CHAPTER

It takes the three of us to right Liebchen, then I have to use the throttle to blast her out of the ditch.

"Here," says the ranger, handing me one of Leibchen's blinkers, "I ride a BMW. This is worth plenty." Then he informs us that there are no campsites at this end of the park. We'll need to back-track 15 miles.

WE MAKE it to Soledad well past dark, weave through the dozen or so pickup trucks and low riders roaring up and down the main street, then check into the first motel

A local rider finds peace and tranquility touring Humboldt County's Redwood State Park in northern California near U.S. Route 101.

we see. The next morning something is wrong with my back. "Probably pulled your *latissimus dorsi* in that ditch," Eddie says. "You need to do some stretching, immediately."

"Thank you Dr. Quinn. Are you gonna help me up or not?"

We bind Liebchen's exposed blinker wires with surgical tape from the first-aid kit, check her fluids, eat a huge breakfast, then resume adventuring. By mid-morning we're rolling through King City, where the air smells of ripe tomatoes. We pass an army of laborers harvesting the fields of ripening fruit. If I were out there, bent over, sweating from sunup to sundown and a couple of geeks on a new BMW honked and waved, I'd bean them with the biggest tomatoes I could find. Then I notice Eddie is waving and the workers are smiling and waving back. So, I lay on the horn.

At first glance, the pinkish jumble of spires, ramparts, and domes at the Pinnacles resembles a mini-version of Utah's eroded sandstone cliffs. But the Pinnacles are not sandstone; they are the remains of an ancient volcano. Most of the rock here is rhyolite that is shot through with volcanic glass, which gives the rock a sparkle and makes it sound hollow. Unlike granite or the dark basaltic volcanic rock found in many parts of the western United States, the rock here poses a unique challenge to climbers because it's weak. Climbers take extra precautions because what initially feels like a toe or finger hold can give way and turn into projectile rock. I am happy we have no climbing gear. Instead, we spend the day in the blazing sun, stripped to our shorts, jogging up and down the dusty, rock-strewn trails that wind through the park. We gulp water from our platypus bladders, explore caves, use our compass for laughs, and generally kill ourselves trying not to be the first one to quit hiking. None of this seems to help my back. Ed keeps calling out from places high above where I can't see him.

"Ed!" I yell. "People come here to enjoy the quiet! And you're probably some place you shouldn't be anyway!"

"We have the Pinnacles to ourselves," he yells back.

"Guess again, bro," someone says, coming down the trail. Three college kids from San Luis Obispo—Tom, Nathan, and Ryan—have been climbing on the rock all day. They're loaded down with gear and one of them is carrying a massage table on his back.

"It's a bouldering mat," Ryan says, throwing it to the ground, then falling hard on it, "in case you fall while bouldering." The mat is placed on the ground while you climb, and hopefully where you'd land if you fall. I'm guessing you shouldn't climb higher than you'd care to fall when bouldering, mat or no mat.

"Who's the goat boy up there doing the bushwhacking?" Nathan says, pointing to Eddie.

"I don't know," I say. "We should call the ranger."

Eddie joins us, and Tom, Nathan, and Ryan give us the beta, the inside skinny on the sport of rock climbing. They've been climbing for two years. Finger strength, toe holds, fist jams, quick draws, bolts, cams, overhangs, and dyno moves are discussed briefly.

"And of course it's a head game," Ryan says. "Sometimes you have to ignore your natural survival instincts and remind yourself you're having fun."

I ask them what they get out of this sport. "It gets us high," Tom says. "Your life is in your own hands, and when you make it to the top you've not only conquered the rock, you've conquered your fear."

"Major high," Ryan adds.

The way my back feels I'd just as soon sit in a lawn chair and watch. Tom says they'll be back at sun up and they have extra climbing gear we can use. Goat Boy and I head back to camp and cook a dozen hot dogs and a can of ranch-style beans as the sun disappears.

Finally, it cools off. Relief turns into curiosity when the temperature continues to drop, then I am alarmed. Around 2 a.m., the inside of Area 51, our fancy new tent, feels like a meat locker. Trying to save space, I'd brought a small, fleece sleeping bag endorsed by Sir Edmund Hillary and sold at Sears. I might as well have used a sheet from the motel.

Ed took saving space one step further and insisted on bringing a wilderness survival blanket. "It retains 80 percent of

A hiker can lose all sense of time during a peaceful walk along the Oregon coast.

Proving that guys do look at maps, father and son find the way and count the miles along the rugged coastline near Kirk Creek in California.

body heat and it fits in my pocket," he'd boasted. Now, he not only looks like a baked potato, he's sweating like one, and, of course, the sweat freezes his body. An hour before sunrise, we eat the remaining hot dog buns. Ed forces me to stretch, then we go see what those climbers are having for breakfast. Fortunately Tom, Nathan, and Ryan are also into eating. They feed us eggs, toast, pasta, coffee, and a Snickers candy bar. I like this sport already.

It's about a 30-minute hike up a trail of switchbacks to the Discovery Wall, a giant, curb-like outcropping that offers a host of climbing routes with varying degrees of difficulty. The climb chosen for today looks to be 75 or 100 feet of vertical rock with a cleft up the middle. Ed and Ryan continue up the path. They'll secure a rope at the top, rappel down, and then use the rope to belay the climbers. I'm looking for some shade when Nathan says, "You go with them, take the extra rope. Just in case."

I hustle up the goat trail and spend the next 20 minutes searching hell's half acre for them. I finally hear Ryan, off to my right, yelling to Nathan. "I'm up here! You're down there, now how about some cooperation! Is the rope long enough or what?" Turns out, Ryan and Nathan are brothers.

By the time I reach them, Ed's tied in and leaning backwards preparing for his first rappel. There's a funny look in his eyes. I peek over the ledge. I can't see Nathan, Tom, or the bottom.

"Maybe I should go first," I say, feeling dizzy. Ed ignores me and starts down, his eyes glued to Ryan, who's coaching him: "That's it, try to relax a little and make sure you don't let go with your right hand."

"That's gonna confuse him," I think. Ed disappears and when he's out of earshot Ryan tells me about the guy who panicked while rappelling here. "He managed to flip himself upside down and then he froze," Ryan says. "It took four of us to haul him back up." I hear Tom and Nathan congratulating Ed so I guess he made it. Ryan rappels commando style which leaves me up here without a harness. By the time I walk back down, Ed's half way up the cleft. Tom is belaying him and shouting encouragement, "Look, step, breathe. That's it, nice move, dude."

I plop down in the shade on the bouldering mat with Nathan. Nathan was climbing barefoot yesterday and fell about 20 feet before his last bolt stopped him. He lost a patch of skin on the ball of his foot. "Papa didn't rappel?" he says to me.

Ed makes it three quarters of the way up before his arms give out. "He's a natural," Tom confides, as he feeds Eddie slack to return to terra firma. Ed's completely drained but his brush with danger has left him crazed. "Did you see me!" he yells, fumbling to free himself from the climbing harness.

"Look at the time," I say, struggling to my feet. "We should get rolling.

There's something we need to do before nightfall."

We head north to Salinas, birthplace and resting place of author John Steinbeck. Champion of the underdog, Steinbeck was branded a communist after releasing *The Grapes Of Wrath*, a heart-wrenching depiction of the plight of migrant workers during the Great Depression. The fruit and vegetable fields we've ridden past were the settings used in the book. We park next to the wrought-iron "Steinbeck" sign that points to his grave. Someone has arranged blue, pink, green, and yellow glass jewelry around the small brass plate—"John Steinbeck, 1902-1968." No mention of his Pulitzer Prize.

Heading north on 101, we pass double trailer rigs loaded down with produce that's stacked way too high for our riding safety. As we squeeze by, diesel fumes mingle with the smell of fresh avocados, lettuce, beets, broccoli, radishes, and artichokes—all the things most children refuse to eat—except for Ed. I could throw him in the back of a turnip truck and he'd eat his way to safety.

We buy sleeping bags at an army surplus store near Prunedale, then hook up with the coastal highway and follow

After many days and miles perched on the back of a motorcycle, Eddie wakes up at Kirk Creek campground in California exhausted, but eager for another day's ride.

the bright, breezy beaches to Santa Cruz. It is a coastal town that people the world over imagine when they think of California, especially people who have seen those wacky beach-blanket, surf's-up, hot-rod films from the 1960s. Santa Cruz has somehow remained in a time warp—beautiful beach, groovy board-walk, big surf (wear a wet suit, the water's

a bit nippy up here) and a strong surfing culture that still "does its own thing," so to speak. "Dude" is still used as a noun, proper noun, adjective, adverb, exclama-tion, or any combination of the above, but "bro" seems to be gaining acceptance.

The attendants at the service station in town help us mail souvenirs home. They fawn over Liebchen—actually

LEFT / Windsurfer heaven is Rooster Rock State Park on the Oregon side of the Columbia River. Windsurfers attach their smallest sails to tackle winds of up to 65 miles per hour. ABOVE / Chris Kelly, owner of Storm Warning demonstrates expert technique in the unforgiving wind and water.

referring to her as "one boss hoss." Monster surf music is blasting from the service bays. When I pay for the gas, I ask the 20-something attendant in sun-bleached dreadlocks, "Do you know the way to San Jose? I'm going back to find some peace of mind, in San Jose."

"Take 17 North, bro."

The traffic out of Santa Cruz angers me so much that I am still fuming at Half Moon Bay where the jagged coastline along Route 1 restores my spirits. I bang my helmet against Ed's to wake him up.

"I'm starving," he yells.

We pull into the tiny seaside town of Montara where we decide to treat ourselves to a big night out. We may feel great but at this point in our journey, we don't smell so great. A shower is in order, and if a bed overlooking the ocean and a fancy restaurant meal are part of the deal—so be it.

The next morning we push north to the Imperial City of the Golden State, San Francisco—or, if you enjoy seeing its citizens cringe, call it "Frisco." Frisco is the most beautiful city in the U.S.A. If you could somehow chop the population in half, roll back the cost of living to 1950s prices, and not think about "the big one"—the earthquake that could hit at anytime—it would be a wonderful place to raise a family.

Also, automobiles should be out lawed in the city. In a "motorcycles only" haven, I wouldn't be forced to do what I'm doing now—lane splitting, which is legal in California and many third-world countries. Lane sharing, as Californians prefer to call it, means a cyclist can ride between lanes of slow moving traffic. Gridlock in Golden Gate Park, and peer pressure from other motorcyclists, has us rolling between lanes of stop-and-go traffic. I think Liebchen is enjoying this more than we are. Many drivers don't seem to care that lane sharing is legal. The lanes open up inside the General Douglas MacArthur Tunnel and the sudden roar tells me to grab some throttle or become someone's hood ornament. We pop out into the blinding sunlight on the Golden Gate Bridge, three abreast with the traffic, where a gust of wind threatens to slap us into an RV. Next exit, Sausalito— sounds like a good place to call the hang-gliding people.

Even the panhandlers in Sausalito prove to be knowledgeable and honest. At a pay phone in front of a grocery store, a gentlemen I take to be a college professor with a big back-pack points out that Liebchen is fuel injected. I should stop trying to find the petcock to turn the fuel on and off. Then he asks me for a spare dollar

so he can get a beer. Such honesty should always be rewarded. "Here's two bucks," I say, "make it a tall." He comes out of the store clutching a beer the size of an oil can and as he moseys off he calls out over his shoulder, "If you're heading north, do not miss the rain forest on the Olympic Peninsula!"

A PILOT'S license will only confuse you when learning to hang glide. Pull back the yoke in a Cessna, you go up. Pull back the control arm on a hang glider, you go

An early start rewards Pat and Ed Kelly with the pleasure of a quiet ride through the morning mist in northern California.

High Peaks in California's Pinnacles
National Monument are the remains of an
ancient volcano—and a climber's paradise.

Embarrassing. Bohdi says it's time to get Ed up here for his lesson. "Wind's picking up," he says. Fine. So is the chopper traffic.

Landing on water is even more fun than taking off from the drink, at least the way Bohdi does it—slip, dive, then pull up (by pushing forward) to glide over the surface for a few seconds and *kerplink*—nary a splash. (I still think Eddie's lesson was 15 minutes longer than mine.)

Early the next morning, a stiff, chilly, sea breeze slaps us around as we motor past the grassy flatlands and chaparral ridges of Point Reyes National Seashore. Liebchen is sporting a new pair of blinkers and feeling frisky after an oil change. For now, Highway 1 is clear of traffic, the road surface is excellent, and the curves ahead—plentiful. Ed wakes up as we power into a tight sweeper overlooking the ocean and Liebchen gobbles up the twisting Sonoma coastline to Bodega Bay, the setting for Alfred Hitchcock's film, *The Birds*. We head inland a few miles to the hamlet of Bodega to visit the schoolhouse, one of the last remaining buildings used as a set in the 1963 film. Just as in the movie, I can still see Tippi Hedron and Suzanne Pleshette having a conversation out in the playground. The monkey bars behind them are empty. Close-ups of the actresses follow, then each time the camera cuts to a two shot, more and more birds are silently perched behind them until the jungle gym is dripping with malevolent black ravens. The movie gives us no scientific reason why our feathered friends have turned on us, but they do—sending the schoolchildren screaming down the road as the birds try to peck their eyes out. That's moviemaking.

The schoolhouse is now a private residence. We take turns out front posing for the camera as if we're being attacked by birds. After the film's developed we'll add the birds in with a Sharpie.

We've seen hundreds, if not thousands, of Harley Davidsons roaring up and down the coast the past few days. Ask Harley riders why they ride a Harley and they'll tell you it's all about soul, tradition, and camaraderie, which evidently includes being as loud as possible, wearing fringed chaps, and ignoring any motorcycle that is not a Harley Davidson. That's a lot of peer pressure to haul around.

It turns out we're on hand for the annual Harley ride through the redwoods. We get in line and follow the horde north through Mendocino and Humboldt Counties to Redwood National Park. The redwoods in this park are the last remaining stretch of old-growth forest, which at one time covered over two million acres of northern California and Oregon. Some of these behemoths are well over 300-feet tall—they could shade the Statue of Liberty—and are the tallest living creatures on Earth. With the last rays of sunlight creating a strobe effect as we

SCENIC AND HISTORIC—U.S. ROUTE 101

The Golden Gate Bridge can be seen from one of the many overlooks along U.S. 101.

U.S. 101 IS ONE OF THE MOST HISTORIC AND SCENIC HIGHWAYS IN NORTH AMERICA. Loosely following the Pacific Coast from southern California to Olympia, Washington, it is a ride that can be enjoyed for a short distance or its entire length of more than 1,300 miles.

Although commissioned in 1926 as one of America's original highways, U.S. 101's history is much older. The road follows the 1769 route of Gaspar de Portola and Father Junipero Serra. It eventually connected 21 missions from San Diego to Sonoma. The trail became known as El Camino Real, The King's Highway.

Between Los Angeles and San Francisco the highway travels through small towns, national forests, past military installations, and rich agricultural fields, with many fantastic views. North of San Francisco the road escapes the bustle of the city for vast stretches. High cliffs, scenic overlooks, tight switchbacks, and endless corners compete for the tourist's attention. The traffic can be intimidating. Motorcyclists should watch out for meandering motor homes, sudden stops, and other throttle-happy motorcyclists.

Once in Oregon, the forest becomes as magnificent as the ocean. Here the highway can lead a traveler in and out of sunshine, fog, drizzle, or hard rain in the space of a few miles. The character of the road changes even more in Washington where the wildlife outnumbers people. Jogging inland several times, U.S. Route 101 passes through forests time has forgotten. The road finally loops back around on itself at the Olympic Peninsula, where in addition to Pacific beaches and rain forest, glacier-covered mountains are part of the landscape. All in all, U.S. 101 is a motorcyclist's dream ride.

PHOTO BY CATHERINE KARNOW

roll through these giants, the overall feeling is almost spiritual, cathedral-like, if you ignore all the motorcycle noise.

We set up camp in the dark among the giant redwoods. The beam of my flashlight keeps catching these striped squirrels or chipmunks closing in as we unpack. What are they doing up at this hour? As I kneel to unroll a ground cloth, one of them scares the life out of me by jumping on my shoulder, then skittering away. Ed swears it was a vampire bat.

Our new sleeping bags are a vast improvement, and as the roar of the Harleys echoes through the forest, I drift off and dream that Ed and I are running down the road while being attacked by chrome-plated thunder chickens.

MY FACE shield is dripping, my boots and gloves are soaked, and water is running across the road, but I've been assured this is not rain we're riding through. It's only the marine layer, the thick blanket of fog that creeps in from the ocean. Welcome to the Oregon coast: rugged, lush, and scenic to the point that we don't mind being wet. Giant sea stacks that resemble castles or sculpture by Roger Dean loom past the surf. Yellow and purple wildflowers, shaggy ferns, and dense forest roll past.

The fog plays tricks on your eyes and your ears. It's hard to tell where sounds are coming from and I think this spooky, Stephen King mist has found its way into Liebchen's fuel tank. She's

developed hiccups at a certain rpm. We pull into a gas station and discover that Oregon is one of three states where it's against the law to pump your own gas. We wonder what happened, and to whom, to make self service verboten.

Espresso seems to be the drink of choice in these parts. We've ridden past auto parts stores, bait shops, beauty parlors, garages, and notary publics—all offering espresso. The coffee selection at this service station is mind boggling. There are so many levers and buttons and syrupy additives, it takes me three tries to concoct something palatable. I hand Ed his first über caffeine drink. All this napping at speed is wearing on my nerves. Ed says he can't sleep at night because I snore, "not like a human," and he hopes tonight I'll suck our two-man tent straight down my windpipe. As we continue north, he's not only awake, now he wants to have a conversation through our helmets.

We push onward, passing through a string of small coastal towns, each one unique and brimming with characters. At Yachats (pronounced *Yahots*), located between Coos Bay and Otter Rock, a waitress tells us her life's story. She couldn't have been older than 18 but she managed to make her life sound like Homer's *The Iliad* and *The Odyssey,* and Jacqueline Susann's book about showbiz girls, *The Valley of the Dolls,* rolled into one. She related this epic struggle *before* taking our order. Ed didn't seem to mind. With her purple spiked hair,

Cleopatra eyeliner, and nose ring, Ed found her alluring, "in a dangerous kind of way."

I realize now that the entire Oregon coast is pretty much one big scenic overlook and state recreation area. At Tillamook, the land of cheese, trees and ocean breeze, we head inland to Portland, the microbrewery capital of the Northern Hemisphere. Portland is also beautiful, with the Willamette River bisecting the city, plenty of landscaped parks, and snow-capped Mount Hood for a backdrop. We pop out at Troutdale, and continue east along the Columbia River for our most scenic ride yet. If the Columbia River Gorge isn't the most gorgeous real estate in the Pacific Northwest, I don't know what is. Waterfalls cascade down steep, lush forest, road tunnels are blasted out of sheer rock, and the mighty Columbia River widens as as we roll along. Across the water, Washington sprawls majestically, more prime real estate. In the 1800s, explorers Lewis and Clark must have thought they'd hit the jackpot when they came through here. "Wait till the Prez hears about this!" Of course now it's more like the Winnebago and logging-truck trail, with the added hazard of serious wind gusts.

I feel like we've been in a wind tunnel with someone evil at the controls since Portland. My nerves are shot, my forearms have seized up, and the spasms originating in my lower back ripple up to my scalp, causing me to accelerate at

inopportune moments. "What are you doing?" Eddie yells.

"Dying, and I'm taking you with me!"

Mercifully, we make it to the town of Hood River around dusk. Hood River is mecca to windsurfers the world over and Liebchen is the only vehicle in town not hauling windsurfing gear. We pull into a motel with a banner out front

that reads, "Welcome Windsurfers!" and in tiny lettering below, "no windsurfing gear allowed in rooms."

My throttle hand is curled into an arthritic claw. Once we get to our room Eddie helps me with the straps, buckles, zippers, snaps, and velcro seams on my riding gear. I toss him my wallet. "Find food, bring back."

The next morning, I call one of the local windsurfing outfitters. After a brief conversation they suggest we take a lesson.

Hanging out 1,300 feet above San Francisco Bay, photographer Miguel Fairbanks (in red helmet) receives an aqua-gliding lesson. The glider is a hybrid aircraft using a 68-hp Rotax engine mounted behind the seats.

Sea breezes and ocean sounds caress the senses and accentuate the vista at a coastal overlook of cliffs at Pescadero State Beach, north of Santa Cruz, California.

PHOTO BY CHARLES GURCHE

Today's windsurfing class consists of Ed, myself, and a gangly 20-year-old also named Patrick. Our instructor, Erin, is a young girl. Now I can look like a complete spastic in front of a girl half my age *and* spend the day trying to control my language. Darnit to heck!

Erin drives us to a "sheltered" cove where I nearly break my neck trying to help unload the sails from the van. The wind is relentless. Set down your wallet, or swim trunks, and they're gone. I'm told the serious wind doesn't arrive until winter. I look up the river and see barge traffic plowing through a colorful forest

Carl Brenner, an employee at Pinnacles National Monument in Pacine, California, explores a talus cave that is formed by fallen boulders undercut by rain and river flow.

of sails frolicking in the whitecaps. For the first time I entertain the idea that wind surfers are out of their minds.

We look dashing in our wet suits. (I'm wearing a back brace under mine.) Erin sets up the simulator, a full windsurfing rig that rotates on a stand like a weather vane. She runs through the basics: how to climb on, pull up the sail, control the boom, and come about. There's only one pointy end on these boards so unless you're planning to travel to the source of the river, you'll need to turn around sooner or later. We take turns on the simulator. I'm pleased to see that Patrick is a complete klutz. My turn comes and the instant I move my sail from the neutral position, I spin around and get pitched into the dirt.

"Damned wind!"

We take our act into the water and, surprisingly, all three of us climb onto our boards, stand, and retrieve our sails. Soon we're raging along at crawl speed. Now what? "Excellent!" Erin says, as she glides past.

Eddie veers off and manages to stay up for the next 20 minutes by slowly and methodically doing everything he just learned on the simulator. Honor student show off. The two Pats stay locked to each other, heading for the weeds. "We should probably turn around before we run out of water," Patrick mumbles.

"Follow me," I say, "Uh!"—*Thump*—*Splash*.

"You're doing fine!" Erin yells from across the cove.

The sail weighs a ton when it's full of water and you'd better be careful which way it's pointing when you haul it back up or the wind will snatch it from your grasp —*Thump*—"Damn!"—*Splash*.

"You're gettin' it!" Erin says.

I can feel river mud squishing around my back brace and these weeds are sharp as sugarcane. Patrick is still up and heading back across the cove. "You better run away!"

So it goes for most of the lesson: "Jeez!" *Splash*.

"Attaboy!"

"You sorry s-- -- - ----h!" *Splash*.

"Good one! Now, try letting go of your sail before it drags you under!"

Near the end of our lesson I finally make it across the cove and back. Oh yeah, it's the little things in life. I'm feeling a glimmer of accomplishment when I look up—here comes Pat—12 o'clock and closing.

"Which way are you going?" he yells, pointlessly.

"Which way the wind's blowing, Einstein!" I answer. *Crunch—Splash, SPLASH*! I lie on my board, sail in the water, and let the wind push me to shore.

Later, we watch the big dogs at Doug's Beach perform. There must be a hundred windsurfers out there mixing it up and when they go down, they go down hard, but somehow they pop back up like corks.

"They're doing acrobatics," Eddie says. "Catching some air."

"Oh." Speaking of, there's a newer water thrill at the Gorge—kite boarding. Strap a big skateboard to your feet, attach an arched parasail to yourself and with a fraction of the wind it takes to windsurf, you're airborne, bro. I could make a splash in this sport.

The next morning we pay 50 cents to cross into Washington on the Bridge of the Gods, a cantilever design that uses steel grating for the road surface. You can look down and see the river rushing by and enjoy the wiggly sensation of riding over steel grates.

Following the advice of the panhandler in Sausalito, we decide to check out the rain forest in Washington's Olympic National Park. At Olympia we ride north along the Olympic Peninsula's

western rim. Seattle and Puget Sound are due east and a world away. This is the west of the Pacific Northwest, 2,000 square miles of sparsely populated wilderness that has it all—a beautifully rugged, fog-shrouded coastline with booming surf you can feel in your bones, pristine lakes and rivers running through lowland, montane and sub-alpine forests. It has alpine meadows leading to glaciers, the snowcapped peak of Mount Olympus, and, we hope, a really cool rain forest.

We turn off U.S. Route 101 and follow the winding road inland about 20 miles to the Hoh Rain Forest. And guess what? It's raining. Rainfall here is measured in feet, 12 to 14 feet per year. We pay the $10 entrance fee and the park ranger tells us the Spruce Nature Trail is closed. A female Roosevelt elk is on the rampage and she's holding two park rangers hostage as we speak. "Cornered," is actually the term the ranger used.

We drop anchor at the Visitors Center and a miracle occurs: The Rain Has Stopped. Sunshine is cutting through the dense canopy. We shed our slimy riding gear and follow the Hoh River Trail into the rain forest. It's positively primordial here, every inch of space is covered with life. Moss, ivy, and giant ferns rise from the forest floor next to 300-foot Sitka spruce trees as wide as a double garage. Douglas firs, red cedars, vine maples, and black cottonwoods all drip with moss and epiphytes, plants that grow on top of other plants. Waterfalls tumble down from the tangled heights, and the whitewater of the Hoh River is a stone's throw away. The water is cold, clear, and swift—snowmelt from Mount Olympus on high. "Keep an eye peeled for Hobbits and Ewoks," I tell Ed.

Ed's not listening. He's running wild, swinging a curved stick he found on the

trail, lost in his *Last of The Mohicans* fantasy. I prefer to stroll purposefully through this paradise.

I realize now that we should have ridden straight to this rain forest and spent at least a week here camping, hiking, and meditating. As it is, we have less than 24 hours to make it back to California to return Liebchen to her rightful owners. I can already tell what a sloppy, choked-up scene that's going to be. My thoughts come to a screeching halt when Eddie ambushes me from behind. "Who's hungry?" he says, waving his stick.

Too tired to cook, Pat and Eddie watch the fire and listen to the surf at Kirk Creek Campground, Big Sur, California.

Riders casting long shadows signal the end of another day cruising the Pacific Coast Highway.

With the 20,320-foot summit of Mount
McKinley, North America's highest mountain, behind them, climbers descend along
the mountain's knife edge. An unarrested
fall could result in a 9,000-foot slide.

DESIRE

CHAPTER SIX

AND ICE

BY DAVID BRILL / PHOTOGRAPHS BY BILL HATCHER

HIGH CAMP at 17,200 feet on Alaska's Mount

McKinley, known to most mountaineers by its Athapascan name, Denali, is one of the Earth's least hospitable places. Due to the windchill factor, nighttime temperatures can plunge to minus 50°F, even during the relatively warm spring and summer climbing season. Frequent storms blowing in off the Gulf of Alaska from the southwest pack 100-mile-per-hour winds and dump massive amounts of snow. These legendary storms can pin down climbers for a week or longer in a brutal holding pattern that can shred tents, dash summit dreams, and transfigure mountaineering from a sport into a fight for survival.

But the mountain's reputation for frigid temperatures didn't seem to faze our camp neighbor and Mount McKinley celebrity Dave Johnston. While my six climbing mates and I shuffled around clad in multiple layers of fleece and down, Johnston, 59, a towering redhead, had stripped off his shirt and was cultivating a tan as he fortified snow walls around his tent.

When we arrived here last night from camp at 14,200 feet, we too had fortified walls, logging more than two hours of gulping air while leveling tent platforms with our ice axes, hewing blocks of snow from the surrounding glacier, and stacking them to a height of five feet around

LEFT / Low on the Kahiltna Glacier, a well-worn trail, which can disappear under fresh snow, leads to base camp on McKinley. ABOVE / Guide Kent Wagner leads his rope team toward high camp at 17,200 feet along the West Buttress.

our tents. This would become part of a nightly ritual that afforded us protection against Mount McKinley's harsh winds.

Johnston was part of a team of climbers who, in 1967, made the first winter ascent to the 20,320-foot summit of this mountain. Johnston's feat is chronicled by Art Davidson in his book *Minus 148*, named for the estimated windchill Johnston and two teammates experienced while wedged into a tiny snow cave at 18,200 feet for six days. By some estimates, they suffered the harshest conditions ever endured by humans on a mountain. The experience changed Johnston's definition of cold.

"People back home in Talkeetna thought we were crazy to come up here when the vegetables were growing at home," he said about this May climb, grinning, as he wiggled a two-foot cube of ice into place in the wall.

If there was anything more out of context here in the palace of the ice gods than Johnston's bare torso, it was his climbing partners. While Johnston carefully cut and stacked snow blocks, his wife, Cari, and 11-year-old son, Galen, were ensconced in their tent, resting, taking in food and fluids, and fortifying themselves for their summit push.

If Galen, an Alaskan-born fifth grader, reached the top, he would become the youngest climber to ascend Mount McKinley and would enter the history books alongside his father. Our group and the Johnston family represented two of the more than 30 climbing teams

sheltered by snow walls here at Mount McKinley's high camp.

While Johnston toiled away effortlessly, my teammates and I struggled against the lethargy that afflicts many at this elevation. Here at 17,200 feet, we were 3,120 feet and 8 hours from the summit. But even the short 100-yard trek to the ledge of granite boulders that edges the high-camp basin left us gasping for breath.

We had been on the mountain 19 days. From the edge we peered down nearly 10,000 feet and could discern the tiny clusters of dome tents marking the sites of our five earlier encampments and our progress up the mountain along the Kahiltna Glacier. Like 80 percent of the climbers on Mount McKinley, we were following the West Buttress Route, identified by Bradford Washburn from aerial photographs. The route is rated Grade II in an Alaskan system that tops out at Grade V in terms of danger and difficulty. It may be easy by Alaskan mountaineering standards, but it marked the ultimate challenge for the seven climbers on our team.

We were primarily middle-age dads and urban professionals, ranging in age from 39 to 61. We were all eager to fulfill a climbing dream—but also inexperienced. I am a 45-year-old father of two preteen daughters; my previous adventures—with the exception of two trips to the 14,410-foot summit of Washington's Mount Rainier—involved places whose most notable perils were insect bites and poison ivy.

Photographing our trip was Bill Hatcher, an experienced sportsman and climber. Bill's pursuit of photos in remote places has taken him on expeditions from the Himalaya to the jungles of the Amazon. This was Bill's first time on McKinley.

We had entrusted our hopes and lives to Gary Talcott, 47, the sturdy, compact leader of our trio of guides from Rainier Mountaineering Incorporated (RMI). RMI, based near Mount Rainier in Ashford, Washington, leads climbers to some of the world's notable summits and is one of only six outfitters licensed to guide on Mount McKinley. Gary had been on the summit twice and was planted at 14,200 feet during the 10-day Arctic blast of 1992 that contributed to the deaths of seven climbers as it dumped 60 inches of snow in a 24-hour period.

Joe Horiskey, 50, was another of our RMI guides and a veritable Mount McKinley guru. He has stood on the summit 13 times since he began climbing in Alaska in the 1970s. He had recently left us at 14,200 feet to help a climber from another RMI team back down the mountain to safety.

Kent Wagner, 38, our third guide, reached within a few hundred vertical feet of the summit several years earlier before being forced to retreat because of a struggling client. While we took a rest day here at 17,200 feet, Kent had been asked to assist another RMI team—down to one guide after having lead three of its seven clients off the

Kent Wagner melts snow for the gallon of water each climber drinks per day. Proper hydration reduces risk of frostbite and altitude sickness.

mountain in a two-week period, two because of altitude sickness. Today Kent was making his way to the summit. His presence would help ensure the clients' safety.

Most of us worried about Kent's decision to leave our expedition to round out the other team's attrition-thinned ranks. But then, mountaineering—a competitive sport pursued by hard-driven people—is also often predicated on such self-sacrifice. Though Kent was as skilled and tough as any climber on the mountain, we wondered if his stamina would hold for back-to-back summit days. We felt that without him, Gary would have to make other arrangements to facilitate our bid for the top.

Out of the 1,305 climbers who would attempt Mount McKinley in 2001, 540 were from outside the United States. Yet we were all drawn to this mountain, one of the coveted continental highs known collectively as the "seven summits."

The highest point in North America may be about 9,715 feet short of Everest's summit, but Mount McKinley boasts several features that set it apart from other major peaks. For one, it presents the greatest vertical gain of any mountain on Earth. For another, because it is situated near the Arctic Circle, where low barometric pressure makes air notoriously thin, Himalayan veterans have claimed that Mount McKinley "feels" like a 23,000-foot peak.

The mountain is imposing and beautiful, but it's also deadly. Since the Hudson Stuck team reached the summit in 1913, Mount McKinley has claimed 91 lives, and about 10 percent of those who attempt to climb it suffer frostbite. In an average year, only about half of the mountain's aspirants reach the summit.

From our vantage point at 17,200 feet we glimpsed jagged, ice-caked spires and snow-choked avalanche chutes. Ground-shaking cascades of falling ice had become a familiar element of the mountain's ambience, and we instinctively scanned the surrounding peaks for the plumes of snow that follow the paths of the avalanches. Gray granite outcrops punctuated blinding-white slopes. Fractured glaciers, their veins of hard ice tinged turquoise by the afternoon sun, silently coursed past us on their slow path to the lowlands. Since the expedition had begun, we

Climbers struggle to secure tents during a storm below Kahiltna Pass, where visibility has been greatly reduced.

Cloud caps indicate high winds and dangerous conditions on McKinley's summit. The pilot of a sightseeing aircraft flying over the peak would alert the National Park Service if struggling climbers were spotted.

hadn't seen a single patch of green—or any other living creatures, save for the marauding ravens that pillage insufficiently buried food caches.

Despite the familiar scenery below, we were more inclined to focus on the terra incognita above, and, for many of us, the prospect of climbing higher than we had ever been. As we peered upward, we watched dozens of climbers, spaced in even intervals along 165-foot climbing ropes, ascend the steep-pitched bowl that leads to 18,200-foot Denali Pass, gateway to the summit ridge. From nearly 1,000 feet below, distant climbers looked like tiny beads strung on an invisible thread, moving almost imperceptibly upward. Their ropes, like ours, kept teams of four or five climbers connected. They served as lifelines: Should one climber fall, his ropemates could execute team arrest, digging in with crampons and ice axes, to stop the slide.

Though we all welcomed the rest day after our long, 3,000-foot push from 14,200 feet, we realized that we shouldn't waste days like this one—windless and warm. The forecast radioed in by the National Park Service staff at base camp called for winds to increase to 40 mph by evening and to persist through the next two days. We knew that our guides wouldn't let us go anywhere near the exposed knife edge of the summit ridge in anything but a light breeze, and with good reason: Climbers blown off balance could slide 9,000-foot.

Most of us had dropped 15 pounds or more from hauling heavy loads and from the withering effects of altitude. Yet, despite our wasted leg muscles and need to rest, we realized that our rations of food and fuel were running low, and that tomorrow might be our one and only shot at the summit.

THE APPROACH to Mount McKinley,

begins not with a trek but on a paved airstrip. On May 28, we had gathered at Hudson Air Service on the outskirts of Talkeetna, a sleepy hamlet two hours north of Anchorage. After running through the gear checklist, we boarded single-engine planes for the 45-minute flight to base camp at 7,200 feet on the Kahiltna Glacier.

Our pilot, Jay Hudson, peered through aviator sunglasses at a panel of worn dials and gauges as he tweaked knobs, yanked levers, and turned the crank on our Cessna 185. Once airborne—the plane laboring under the load of three mountaineers, one pilot, and the hundreds of pounds of gear stowed behind our seats—we banked left and bounced on thermals over the Talkeetna River.

I glanced ahead and noticed a narrow notch in the looming wall of mountains that looked like a gunsight. The plane sounded reluctant, tired. A feeble whine had replaced the groaning from the engine, and I measured the

distance to the notch against our slug-
gish ascent. As Jay explained the sober-
ing particulars of One-Shot Pass, my
toes curled involuntarily inside my
boots. When our wingtips cleared the
pass, I relaxed, shifted my focus forward,
and caught my first full glimpse of
Mount McKinley presiding over a court
of lesser peaks. My eyes, shielded by glacier glasses, began to pick out features of
the Arctic expanse below. I saw the tiny
forms of climbers navigating between
and around gaping crevasses and beginning the long slog toward the summit.
Then I saw a sprawling village of tents
marking base camp and, just beyond,
the tracks of ski planes slicing the
Kahiltna Glacier's landing strip.

As we exited the plane, another RMI
team queued up for a return trip to the
world of hot showers, cold beers, and
warm beds. They looked like weary war-
riors, bone thin and with exposed skin
wind-lashed to a brown-red. They were
sullen and silent. Their experience at
17,200 feet was decidedly different from
what ours would be. Pinned in tents for
seven days, hammered by high winds
and extreme temperatures, they never
even got a shot at the summit.

Prior to the trip, each of us had
acquired the mountain of gear listed on

During a rest day at 11,000 feet, Brad Skidmore
and Nat Brace pretend to use a remote control for
a television sculpted from snow.

the three-page, single-spaced equipment checklist provided by RMI. Among the requisite items were multiple layers of clothing, including stout summit parkas, mittens, and hats; snowshoes, crampons, ice axes, carabiners, ascenders, and other pieces of mountaineering hardware; sleeping bags weighing seven pounds each and rated to 40 below zero; and 26 days' worth of personal lunches and snacks. Added to that was the considerable weight of group gear—tents, gallon cans of fuel, enormous cook pots, expedition stoves, shovels, and sufficient food for 26 breakfasts and dinners.

We departed base camp on May 29,

A hot beverage and a moment alone help to fortify Kent Wagner. Emerging from the tent at this elevation of 14,200 feet means facing temperatures that can plunge to well below zero.

hauling more than 100 pounds each, half on our backs, half in the plastic sleds we pulled behind us. We'd pull the sleds—known affectionately among mountaineers as "pigs"—to 14,000 feet, and then leave them because the terrain becomes too steep to tow them farther.

The plan was to "single-carry"—move with our full loads—to 9,600 feet. Then we'd begin double-carrying—dividing our loads—carrying half up and caching them under three feet of snow, then returning to lower camp to sleep. This was a strategy to help us adapt to high altitude.

From base camp we ascended the gentle rise of the lower Kahiltna Glacier, edged by parallel walls of mountains. By midday, temperatures had climbed to 90°F. We stripped down to shirtsleeves and wore bandannas, Foreign Legion style, under our ball caps to protect us from the searing sun. Lest anyone confuse us with skilled mountaineers, we had to stop every 100 feet or so to make adjustments to our pigs or to right them after they had flipped belly up.

I could sense frustration rising in Kent's voice as he called out, "Okay, guys, are we ready?" Once we gave him the nod he settled back into the rest step, a technique of locking the knees with each step to take the strain off muscles and place it on the skeletal system. The rest step, along with pressure breathing, increases efficiency and reduces fatigue. By deeply inhaling and then exhaling through pursed lips to increase pressure in the lungs, it offsets the effects of thin air. Pressure breathing would prove essential higher up.

With Kent rest stepping like a robot in hyperdrive, we soon pulled away from Gary's and Joe's rope teams. Once we stopped for a rest break, Joe let Kent know he wasn't happy about it.

"My God, Kent, you're climbing like a gut-shot cougar!" he said between gasps. "How about slowing down a bit?"

"Okay, Joe," Kent answered, and with that, we pulled off the trail in view of our destination at 7,900 feet, marked by walls left by earlier expeditions.

We spent our second night at 9,600 feet, and on our third day, while descending from our first double-carry, to 11,000 feet, we encountered our first major Mount McKinley storm. As we descended, still an hour from camp, we were enveloped in a blinding blizzard.

The distinguishing features of the landscape vanished, heavy snowfall erased our boot prints, and we were left to navigate by following the green bamboo wands we'd planted in the snow to mark the route on our ascent.

THE STORM cleared, and we reached 11,000 feet the next day, primed for our first rest day on the mountain. We found that other idle climbers had sculpted a television set from snow and placed it on a large snow pedestal. Two bamboo wands served as antennae, and the remote sat on the "coffee table" beside the "couch." We grabbed water bottles and a bag of food and settled onto the ersatz couch to watch baseball, though we couldn't decide whether to cheer for Nat Brace's Seattle Mariners or Brad Skidmore's Cincinnati Reds.

From 11,000 feet, we topped Motorcycle Hill and rounded Windy Corner, a barren ridge of granite scoured clean by near-constant winds. Then we hugged the mountain above a steep drop into a sea of crevasses not far from camp. At one point, Gary motioned us off the trail for a break. In that instant, the snow fell away beneath my boot, and I plunged up to my thigh in a crevasse. As I scrambled to regain my balance, more of the snow bridge broke away, and I peered down into a bottomless crack of blue ice. Gary tightened the rope, and I climbed to safety.

We had ascended from base camp at 7,200 feet to 14,200 feet in nine days, on schedule to nail the summit in just over two weeks. From there, we were only three days short of the top. That would have been under ideal conditions—but the conditions we had for the next several days were far from ideal. We spent more than a week at 14,200 feet due to

Mount McKinley's notoriously fickle weather. Just as our interminable bivouac was ending and we were preparing to move upward, the weather report came in over the radio: If the park service predictions proved right, the winds would top out at over 100 miles per hour in the next couple of days. If the worst-case scenario played out, we

LEFT / Subtle colors emerge in twilight from the base of Motorcycle Hill at 11,000 feet, looking toward Mount Foraker. ABOVE / Brad Skidmore sets his crampon points carefully as he descends an 800-foot section of steep snow—the most technical stretch of the West Buttress Route.

would face a storm that rivaled the 10-day blow of 1992—one of the deadliest storms in Mount McKinley's history.

"Guys, the park service is really concerned about the storm," Gary said. "Some teams are attempting to summit, but there have been a lot of cases of frostbite. We're staying put for the time being. We've been here longer than anyone expected, and

you guys are dealing with the toughest aspect of mountaineering—the mental part. But we're all strong and healthy, we have plenty of food and fuel, and I think we all have a shot at the summit."

Joe, who over his months spent on the mountain had seen just about everything, paused to reflect on our situation: "Ah, hell," he said, scratching a two-week growth of stubble. "No big deal."

Climbers descend the steep snow couloir, or gully, from the top of the West Buttress to the wide plateau at 14,200 feet.

We responded to Gary's cautious assessment with a collective groan. We'd been stuck there long enough to regard ourselves as the official Camp 14,200 Welcome Wagon. In that time we'd conversed with a group of policemen dubbed "Cops on Top," who were hauling a plaque up the mountain to honor a colleague killed in the line of duty. Then there was Mike Gajda, a ski patroller from Whistler, British Columbia, whom we called "The Crazy Canadian." Mike seemed more determined to ski than to summit. Over the previous days, we had grown accustomed to seeing his lone figure ascend impossibly steep slopes and

Stout snow walls protect the team's four expedition tents from high winds. To the right, 17,400-foot Mount Foraker, the second highest peak in the Alaska Range, dominates the horizon.

then schuss back down, slicing across opening crevasses and negotiating the fine lines between skiing and falling.

We'd watched countless other climbing teams set out in marginal conditions only to stagger back down, beaten, exhausted, and eager to return home—forget the summit.

"We want you to go home with all the fingers and toes you arrived with," Gary had added, attempting to dampen our obvious disappointment.

"I need these fingers," said Ken Coffee, owner of an Oklahoma-based engineering firm and one of my two tent mates. "I just bought a new guitar."

WE AROSE on June 13, our 16th day on the mountain, to clear skies and drifting snow. Gary told us we were heading up. Our luck had returned, or so we thought.

By 10 a.m., we were roped up and crunching snow toward high camp at 17,200 feet. Ahead of me on the rope, Clay Howard, a former college athlete now in his early 50s and one of the fittest members of our team, stopped abruptly and leaned on his ice axe. I could see his chest heaving. He called out to Kent, who led the rope, in a frail voice. "I'm not feeling so good," he said.

"Clay, take a few minutes," Kent said. We waited five.

"You ready, Clay?" Kent asked.

"Yeah, I think so."

The rope pulled tight, and we began moving. Within a few minutes, Clay stopped again.

Kent jettisoned his pack, unclipped from our rope, and rushed downslope to take the load off Clay's shoulders. Our progress upward stopped there, and the guides began to reveal the decision-making savvy they're noted for, though most of the rest of us knew what was coming. There's only one cure for altitude sickness: For Clay, the trip was over. He would be led back down the mountain to safety.

"This kind of problem can hit anybody at any time," Gary said. "The route from here is tough, and we're only a couple of hours into an eight-or-nine-hour day. If you're feeling sick here, you probably will only feel worse the higher you go."

"Maybe if I rest here awhile, I'll feel better," Clay said. "I don't want to mess things up for the rest of the group."

Then Kent intervened. Not known for his light touch, he pursued a different—and decidedly less subtle—tack.

"Clay, if you're hurting here, there's no way you're going to make it to high camp," he said. "You have to go down."

Clay would be escorted down by another RMI guide the next day.

An hour later, we arrived back in purgatory. "Hey, something about this place looks familiar," said Brad, a neurosurgeon in his early 40s from northern Kentucky. After dumping his pack, he approached me and offered his professional medical assessment: "As tough as this is on Clay, there's really no other option. Maybe he'd be okay in a day or two, but the guides have to think about what's best for the expedition."

By noon the next morning, Clay was escorted down and our number had been reduced to seven clients. We were back at 15,400 feet, peering up at an 800-foot section of snow and hard ice pitched at what seemed to be a 65-degree angle—the most technical stretch of the West Buttress Route. We'd attach our mechanical ascenders onto the fixed lines anchored into the snow. The ascenders, tied into our harnesses, would slide freely as we moved up, but grab should we take a fall. I'd been dreading this stretch since I first began planning my trip. As it turned out, my concerns were justified.

Years earlier, while interviewing Dick Bass, the first man to climb the highest peak on each continent, I learned the value of humor—and especially of being able to laugh at yourself—in negotiating tight spots on big mountains. Webster's dictionary defines humor as "the mental faculty of discovering, expressing, or appreciating the ludicrous or absurdly incongruous." The scene on the headwall at 15,400 feet had all the right elements. I was perched on a steep slope that might have served as the ramp for the Olympic ski jump. My 60-pound pack was biting into my shoulders. The front points of my crampons had a precarious hold on a near-vertical bulge of hard ice.

I was certain that I would enjoy a good belly laugh when I fully grasped the "absurdly incongruous" qualities of a neophyte mountaineer and middle-age father of two clinging to the side of one of the world's great peaks. But the only emotions I registered at the moment were fear and a needling sense of inadequacy. My ice axe kept ricocheting off the surface as if it were cast from hardened steel, while my right hand gripped the mechanical ascender attached to the fixed line. Ahead of me on the rope, Kent, possibly the toughest human being I'd ever met, offered me gentle encouragement when the perverse process of multitasking in a strange and threatening environment inclined me to freeze.

"You *MUST* keep up," he shouted over the wind and blowing snow.

The only thing that frightened me more than sliding off the mountain was angering Kent, so I redoubled my efforts, hammered my ice axe into a crack, and began pulling myself up.

So far, the scene clearly contained incongruous elements. Then fate added the ludicrous part. I felt a sharp tug on the rope from below. I turned to see that

my tent mate Ken Coffee had thrown a crampon and was sliding downslope. He hadn't yet clipped onto the fixed line, so the only thing halting his slide was me, my ascender, and the self-arrest skills of my other tent mate, Nat Brace, a former systems engineer for Microsoft, who was tied into the rope below Ken.

Over the screaming of my Achilles tendons I heard a garbled string of unmentionables shouted from above, before Kent formulated a simple sentence telling us what we already knew.

"We *CAN'T* stop here!" he yelled.

En route to the summit, expedition leader Gary Talcott pushes into a 40-mile-per-hour wind above Denali Pass at just over 18,000 feet.

BRADFORD WASHBURN—DEAN OF MCKINLEY

Bradford Washburn began a life of interest in Mount McKinley after photographing it in 1936.

IN 1936, AFTER FLYING OVER MOUNT McKINLEY TO SHOOT AERIAL PHOTOGRAPHS FOR the National Geographic Society, Bradford Washburn became entranced by Alaska's highest peak. From the earliest mountaineering explorations of Mount McKinley at the turn of the century, until 1951, nearly all expeditions approached the 20,320-foot peak from Wonder Lake, in the north, via the Muldrow and Harper Glaciers. In 1942, after getting a good look at the mountain again, Washburn wrote, "As we spotted the Kahiltna Glacier 10,000 feet below us, we suddenly realized that almost all of that side of McKinley was nothing but a safe, steep, chilly scramble." He described this "technically easy approach" from the west via the upper reaches of the Kahiltna Glacier and the West Buttress. Yet, the lengthy overland hike from civilization to the upper Kahiltna seemed daunting compared with the 35-mile trek from Wonder Lake.

In 1947, Washburn and his wife, Barbara, scaled the mountain to begin gathering data for the Mount McKinley Map, which is still in use. Four years later, Terris Moore, a pilot who had a plane outfitted with retractable skis, flew Washburn and three other climbers to the Kahiltna. They were joined by four others who had trekked in from Wonder Lake. By following the West Buttress Route, the eight climbers reached the summit.

Today, more than 80 percent of the climbers on Mount McKinley follow the West Buttress Route. It is rated an Alaskan Grade II, the scale tops out at Grade V in terms of danger and difficulty making it the safest and easiest route to the top.

PHOTO BY BOB REEVE, NGS

Below me, Nat rushed to Ken's aid and effected a speedy repair. In an interminable two minutes, the tension on the rope eased, and I began to creep upward, convinced that the crisis had passed.

Then it happened again.

As I felt the oddly familiar tug on the rope, I realized that the worst that could happen was a short tumble and badly bruised ego. I finally grasped the humorous qualities of the situation: Above me, a type-A guide bellowed his disapproval. Directly below me, the hapless victim of equipment failure, now seated, kicked with his one cramponed boot against the tug of gravity, like Robert Shaw's character sliding into the gaping maw of the great white shark in *Jaws*. And below him, at least a dozen excited Taiwanese climbers, all wearing identical hats with GORE-TEX stitched across the front, pointed and yammered in Chinese, saying God-knows-what.

As before, Nat helped Ken secure his crampons—this time the repair held—and at last we were moving up to the tight gap at 16,200 feet, and our first rest break in nearly two hours of climbing.

I collapsed into a heap on top of my overturned pack. Exhausted from a short 800-foot scramble, I fully fathomed the strength and technical savvy of the square-jawed icons of the climbing world—Messner, Anker, Ridgeway, Viesturs—who seek out the most challenging routes and avoid the pedestrian paths that lead neophytes like me up big mountains.

By six that evening, we staggered into high camp, huffing in the lean mountain air like a bunch of Lamaze trainees. As the sun dipped behind the western peaks, the temperature began its rapid nightly plunge to minus 20°F. We scattered to our tents, now foul-smelling places crammed with gear, clothing, and anything else we hoped to prevent from freezing.

My tent mate Ken and I inserted headphone buds into our ears and dialed in our favorite radio stations. I opted for the oldies station broadcast from Fairbanks. Meanwhile, Nat studied pictures of his wife and infant son, Clark, and smiled.

Just as I began to drift off to sleep, I pulled the headphones from my ears and heard Kent's familiar voice. He was back from the summit after a long day of climbing. I also heard the wind picking up, pelting the side of our tent with snow. Tomorrow would be our day, provided Kent hadn't run out of gas—and the weather broke.

THE NEXT morning, we dug our way out of our tents through an accumulated two feet of snow, which had blown into the vestibule. Kent was poised over the stoves, seemingly none the worse for wear after covering 6,240 vertical feet in over 12 hours the day before. Gary advised us to hold off on packing our summit gear.

With the summit a day behind them, team members descend from high camp along the rocky, exposed ridgeline of the West Buttress, which offers stunning views of the Alaska Range.

"I think we're going to wait and see what the weather's like tomorrow," said Dave Johnston, now clad in his cold-weather gear, who wandered over to our camp.

It's hard to take issue with a guy who survived a week of minus 148°F. As it turned out, Dave and his family would gain the summit the next day, and 11-year-old Galen would go on to impress his classmates back home with his report on how he spent his summer vacation. Galen looked rosy-cheeked and healthy when we met him at 14,200. Now, at 17,200, he was haggard and pale, much like the rest of us, and had rarely left his tent since he'd arrived.

Throughout the morning, we milled around camp, gulping air, peering up at Denali Pass, wondering if we'd ever get there. Then, at 10:30, Gary called us together.

"The wind is still up, but let's pack our gear and get up to the pass," he said. "This may only be a training climb, but we won't know till we get up there and put our noses in the weather."

We stowed water bottles in our packs, inserted chemical heatpacks into our boots and gloves, made sure goggles and face masks were accessible, cinched tight our crampon straps, donned bulky down summit parkas, and pulled on shells over liner gloves.

By 11:30, we started the slow slog to Denali Pass at 18,200 feet. We arrived in three hours, and a frigid wind belted us in the face. I was expecting Gary to turn us back. Instead, he gathered us together.

"Boys, this is our summit day," he said, grinning.

We climbed past the South Peak's notable landmarks: the weather meter at 18,900 feet and the nob of Archdeacon's Tower at 19,650 feet. We descended into the broad expanse of the Football Field at 19,500 feet, dropped our packs, and began kicking steps to the summit ridge.

Suddenly, the world seemed thoroughly uncomplicated. There was only the rhythmic crunch of my crampons, the rasp of my breath, and the sound of my ice axe piercing snow. I don't recall another moment in my life when my purpose seemed so clear or my goal so close at hand.

I planted my boots on the foot-wide trail of the knife edge, strangely unconcerned that an unarrested fall could result in a 9,000-foot slide. Then I glanced up and saw Gary ahead, reeling me in. As I reached out to shake his hand, I felt warm tears on my cheeks.

The others arrived, and for the next 20 minutes, after the back slapping had ended, we stood silent, savoring the view. It was June 16, 8:30 p.m., minus 20°F, and we were standing on top of North America. As my eyes swept the endless expanse of ragged mountains that sprawled around us, it occurred to me that in the context of 3 weeks of hauling huge loads and waiting out weather and stomping in snow with numb feet, 20 minutes of standing on the highest point of ground wouldn't amount to much— if it didn't mean everything.

For me, Mount McKinley was an end point, not a stepping stone to higher and more celebrated peaks. I'd promised a few folks back home—including my daughters—that once I returned from this mountain, I'd hang up my crampons for good. Therefore, this moment marked a literal and figurative high point in my life. As we began our descent, I reflected, with some sadness, that I would never again stand with steel points in ice and view the world from this vantage point.

Ironically, the full emotional payoff I'd hoped would await me on the summit proved elusive. It's difficult to bask in your success when some 13,120 feet of rough and dangerous terrain lie between where you stand and your safe evacuation from the mountain. As it turned out, the payoff would come much later, over the coming months, as I relived this moment countless times in the shelter of civilization, in the company of family and friends.

We were back at high camp by 11:30 p.m., and I collapsed in the snow. I felt my hands and feet freezing but didn't have the strength to stand. Eventually, I staggered to the tent, slid into my sleeping bag, and lapsed into sleep.

June 16, 8:30 p.m.: A team of middle-age dads and nine-to-fivers stands on top of North America, momentarily basking in success before beginning the perilous descent back.

Two days later, we picked up all the gear we had cached along the way, and approached the landing strip at 7,200 feet, listening to the constant drone of

Below Squirrel Point, at 11,500 feet, the team passes fully-loaded climbers bound for the top. The two-day descent from the summit covers a distance that consumed 20 days on the way up.

departing and arriving planes. Along the way, we'd stopped to chat with a few ascending climbers who had heard over their radios about Kent's back-to-back summit days—a feat that had already earned him the nickname "Do-It-Again Wagner."

We topped a rise, and I saw the tent city marking base camp and a single

approached us with cold beers. The scene was so surreal that I had to resist the impulse to run from her.

A few days later, I was on a plane bound for Tennessee. Once we were airborne, the pilot directed our attention to the snow-cloaked hulk of Mount McKinley, looming off to our left. While middle-aged tourists in Rockport walking shoes muttered and pointed, I settled back into my seat and closed my eyes. I realized all too well that the view out the window couldn't begin to compare with the image of that remarkable mountain fixed forever in my memory.

In the weeks that followed, I began to regard myself as a retired mountaineer with only one notable peak to my credit, though my Mount McKinley experience grows in importance even as it grows more distant in time. I joyfully returned to my daughters, who seem to have forgiven me for leaving them for nearly a month and risking my life for something they can't yet grasp.

They ask me often about the mountain. All I can tell them is that Mount McKinley was a brutish mountain, but more grand and beautiful than any place I've ever seen. I also assure them that I'll never go back. Someday, when they're old enough to understand, I'll explain to them that I traveled to Alaska on some vague, middle-age quest and that, somewhere on that ice-locked summit, I found just what I was looking for.

plane parked on the glacier with Hudson Air painted on the side. Randy, our pilot, was sprawled in a lounger, waiting for us.

Nat, Ken, and I piled into the first plane out, and within 45 minutes of knocking ice off our boots and packs, we were standing on the sun-baked landing strip as a woman wearing shorts

A nearly full moon, suspended in a cobalt
sky, pierces the twilight of Mount McKinley.
During the summer climbing season, the
Alaska Range never goes completely dark.

ADDITIONAL INFORMATION

Below is additional information on the adventures included in this book.

POWDER PASSION

CANADIAN MOUNTAIN HOLIDAYS
P.O. Box 1660
Banff, AB T1L 1J6
(403) 762-7100 / (800) 661-0252
www.cmhski.com

CRESCENT SPUR HELI-SKIING
General Delivery
Crescent Spur, BC V0J 3E0
(250) 553-2300 / (800) 715-5532
www.crescentspurheliski.com/

GREAT CANADIAN HELI-SKIING
P.O. Box 175
Golden, BC V0A 1H0
(250) 344-2326
www.canadianheli-skiing.com

MIKE WIEGLE HELICOPTER SKIING
P.O. Box 159
Blue River, BC V0E 1J0
(250) 673-8381
www.wiegele.com/

PURCELL HELICOPTER SKIING LTD.
P.O. Box 1530
Golden, BC V0A 1H0
(250) 344-5410
www.purcellhelicopterskiing.com/

R.K. HELI-SKI
P.O. Box 695
Invermere, BC V0A 1K0
(250) 342-3889
(800) 661-6060
www.rkheliski.com

ROBSON HELIMAGIC
P.O. Box 18
Valemount, BC V0E 2Z0

(250) 566-4700
www.robsonhelimagic.com/

SELKIRK TANGIERS HELICOPTER SKIING LTD.
P.O. Box 130
Revelstoke, BC V0E 2S0
(250) 837-5378 /(800) 663-7080
www.selkirk-tangiers.com

TETON ESCAPE

IDAHO LLAMA GEAR
1528 East Elk Loop Road
Ashton, ID, 83420
(208) 652-7799
www.llamagear.com/

JACKSON HOLE LLAMAS
P.O. Box 12,500
Jackson Hole, WY 83002
(800) 830-7316
www.jhllamas.com

ON THE LOOSE EXPEDITIONS
1035 Carse Road
Huntington, VT 05462
(800) 688-1481
www.otloose.com

OPPORTUNITY LLAMAS
E3602 1450th Avenue
Ridgeland, WI 54763
(715) 455-1144
www.llamamall.com/opptyllamas

WAYFARING TRAVELER RANCH
P.O. Box 98
1100 Lane 38
Burlington, WY 82411
(307) 762-3536
www.wyomingbnbranchrec.com/Wayfaring.html

DESERT COMMUNION

CANYONLANDS NATIONAL PARK
2282 S. West Resource Blvd.
Moab, UT 84532-3298
(435) 719-2313
Backcountry Reservations (435) 259-4351
www.nps.gov/cany

HOLIDAY EXPEDITIONS
544 E. 3900 South
Salt Lake City, Utah 84107
(800) 624-6323
www.bikeraft.com

KAIBAB MOUNTAIN BIKE TOURS
391 South Main Street
Moab, UT 84532
(435) 259-7423 / (800) 451-1133
www.kaibabtours.com/

POISON SPIDER BICYCLES
497 North Main Street
Moab, UT 84532
(800) 648-1792
www.nicholsexpeditions.com/psb.htm

RIM TOURS
1233 S. Highway 191
Moab, UT 84532
(880) 626-735
www.rimtours.com/

WESTERN SPIRIT CYCLING
478 Mill Creek Drive
Moab, UT 84532
(800) 845-BIKE / (435) 259-8732
www.westernspirit.com/

RIVER WILD

LAUREL HIGHLANDS RIVER TOURS
P.O. Box 107
Ohiopyle, PA 15470
(800) 4-raftin
www.laurelhighlands.com

MOUNTAIN STREAMS OUTFITTERS
P.O. Box 106
Ohiopyle, PA 15470
(800) 723-8669
www.mtstreams.com/

MOUNTAIN SURF
P.O. Box 70,
276 Maple Street
Friendsville, MD 21531
(301) 746-5389
www.mountainsurf.com/

OHIOPYLE STATE PARK
P.O. Box 105
Ohiopyle, PA 15470
(724) 329-8591
(888) 727-2757 Reservations and Information
www.dcnr.state.pa.us/stateparks/parks/ohio.htm

PRECISION RAFTING
P.O. Box 185
Friendsville, MD 21531
(800) 477-3723
www.precisionrafting.com

RIVERSPORT
P.O. Box 95
Confluence, PA 15424
(800) 216.6991
www.shol.com/kayak

SWALLOW FALLS STATE PARK
c/o Herrington Manor State Park
222 Herrington Lane
Oakland, MD 21550
(301)387-6938
www.dnr.state.md.us/publiclands/
western/swallowfalls.html

WHITE WATER ADVENTURERS
P.O. Box 31
Ohiopyle, PA 15470
(800) 992-7238
www.wwaraft.com/

WILDERNESS VOYAGEURS
P.O. Box 97
Ohiopyle, PA 15470
(800) 272-4141
www.wilderness-voyageurs.com/

COASTAL CRUISING

AAA/ CALIFORNIA STATE AUTOMOBILE ASSOCIATION
150 Van Ness Avenue
San Francisco, CA 94102
(800) 937-5523
www.csaa.com/home/

BIG WINDS
207 Front Street
Hood River, Oregon 97031
(888) 509-4210
www.bigwinds.com

HUMBOLDT REDWOODS STATE PARK
P.O. Box 276
Weott, CA 95571
(707) 946-2263
www.humboldtredwoods.org/

OLYMPIC NATIONAL PARK
600 East Park Avenue
Port Angeles, WA 98362-6798
(360) 563-3130
www.nps.gov/olym

PINNACLES NATIONAL MONUMENT
5000 Hwy. 146
Paicines, CA 95043
(831) 389-4485—Visitor Information
www.nps.gov/pinn/

SAN FRANCISCO HANG GLIDING CENTER
No address; by reservation only
(510) 528-2300
sfhanggliding.com

SKYDIVE SANTA BARBARA
Lompoc Airport
1801 North H Street, Suite C
Lompoc, CA 93436
(805) 740-9099
www.skydivesantabarbara.com

DESIRE AND ICE

ALASKA-DENALI GUIDING, INC.
P.O. Box 566
Talkeetna, AK 99676
(907) 733-2649
www.climbalaska.org/

AMERICAN ALPINE INSTITUTE
1515 12th Street
Bellingham, WA 98825
(360) 671-1505
www.mtnguide.com/

DENALI NATIONAL PARK
Superintendent's Office
P.O. Box 9
Denali Park, AK 99755
(907) 733-1016
www.nps.gov/dena/

MOUNTAIN TRIP
P.O. Box 111809
Anchorage, AK 99511
(907) 345-6499
www.mountaintrip.com/

NATIONAL OUTDOOR LEADERSHIP SCHOOL
P.O. Box 981
Palmer, AK 99511
(907) 745-4047
www.nols.edu/

RAINIER MOUNTAINEERING, INC.
P.O. Box Q
Ashford, WA 98304
(360) 569-2227
www.rmiguides.com/

TALKEETNA RANGER STATION
Box 588
Talkeetna, AK 99676
(907) 683-2294
www.nps.gov/dena/

INDEX

ACKNOWLEDGMENTS

POWDER PASSION

Bernadette McDonald wishes to thank Hans Gmoser and Marty von Neudegg of Canadian Mountain Holidays.

José Azel wishes to thank Lili Winslow, Daniel Griffith, and Lyle Ledoux.

TETON ESCAPE

John Murray wishes to express his deeply felt gratitude to Dave and Jill Hodges for their warm hospitality and kindness.

Beth Wald would like to thank Jill and David Hodges, the Llama gurus!

DESERT COMMUNION

Allan Fallow would like to thank: Denice Crall, Rim Tours, Moab, Utah; Robert Devine; Paul Downey, Katie Juenger, and Steve Swanke, all of Canyonlands National Park, Utah, National Park Service; Thomas Dudley, Department of Integrative Biology, University of California/ Berkeley; Poison Spider Bicycles, Moab, Utah; John Randall; Charles Schelz, Biologist, National Park Service, Moab, Utah; Robert H. Webb, U.S. Geological Survey, Tucson, Arizona.

RIVER WILD

Dale Herring would like to thank Jess Whitemore, Ed Gertler, Steve Strothers, Terry Peterson, Joan Herring, Dave Rickers, and Chuck Stump.

COASTAL CRUISING

Pat Kelley would like to thank Roy Oliemuller; Corporate Communications Group; BMW of North America (for lending us Liebchen); Lorenzo Saenz, Manager, Motorcycle Department, BMW of San Fransisco (for repairs to Liebchen); Dave and Margo Thomas, Mag's Bags (for grand touring luggage bag).

Miguel Luis Fairbanks wishes to thank Dave Gutierrez and Chris Kelly; Storm Warning (windsurfing guys from Hood River, and in action at "Rooster Rock" on the Columbia River, OR); Kurt Hess; David Hughes (owner of Skydive Santa Barbara, and the man he jumped with, and who delivered him safely to Earth).

DESIRE AND ICE

David Brill wishes to express heartfelt thanks to Gary, Kent, Joe, and the other guides of Rainier Mountaineering Inc., who lead ordinary men and women to extraordinary places.

Bill Hatcher gives many thanks to the RMI guides—Gary Talcott, Joe Horisky, and Kent Wagner—who did everything to make my shoot a success. Also special thanks to those that helped me train and prepare for the climb—Jim Zellers, Glen Dunmire, Adam Lederer, Gareth Martins, Peter Nobles, John Wason, and Kent Wagner. I want to thank my friends at Black Diamond, Patagonia, The North Face and Osprey Packs for their technical help. I'd like to mention my editor, Dan Westergren, for all his help with this project. A special thanks to my wife, Kate Thompson, who accompanied me on many training runs and joined me in Alaska after the climb.

Photos for Powder Passion by José Azel/ Aurora for National Geographic. Photos for Teton Escape by Beth Wald/ Aurora for National Geographic. Photos for Desert Communion by Peter McBride/Aurora for National Geographic.

ADVENTURE AMERICA

Published by the National Geographic Society

John M. Fahey, Jr.	*President and Chief Executive Officer*
Gilbert M. Grosvenor	*Chairman of the Board*
Nina D. Hoffman	*Executive Vice President*

Prepared by the Book Division

Kevin Mulroy	*Vice President and Editor-in-Chief*
Charles Kogod	*Illustrations Director*
Marianne R. Koszorus	*Design Director*
Barbara Brownell	*Director of Continuities*

Staff for this Book

Dale-Marie Herring	*Project and Text Editor*
Sadie Quarrier	*Illustrations Editor*
Melissa Farris	*Designer*
Sallie Greenwood	*Researcher*
Carl Mehler	*Director of Maps*
Equator Graphics, Greg Ugiansky	*Map Research and Production*
Barbara Brownell, Margo Browning, Patrice Silverstein	*Contributing Editors*
R. Gary Colbert	*Production Director*
Lewis R. Bassford	*Production Project Manager*
Sharon Kocsis Berry	*Illustrations Assistant*
Connie D. Binder	*Indexer*

Manufacturing and Quality Control

Christopher A. Liedel	*Chief Financial Officer*
Phillip L. Schlosser	*Managing Director*
John T. Dunn	*Technical Director*
Vincent P. Ryan	*Manager*
Clifton M. Brown	*Manager*

Library of Congress Cataloging-in Publication Data

Adventure America.
  p. cm.
  ISBN 0-7922-8048-2 (reg.) —ISBN 0-7922-8049-0 (dlx.)
  Includes index.
    1. Outdoor recreation—United States. 2. Outdoor recreation—Canada. 3. Adventure and adventurers—United States.
    4. Adventure and adventurers—Canada. I. National Geographic Society (U.S.)

GV191.4 .A34 2002
790'.097—dc21
                                  2002070312

One of the world's largest nonprofit scientific and educational organizations, the National Geographic Society was founded in 1888 "for the increase and diffusion of geographic knowledge." Fulfilling this mission, the Society educates and inspires millions every day through its magazines, books, television programs, videos, maps and atlases, research grants, the National Geographic Bee, teacher workshops, and innovative classroom materials. The Society is supported through membership dues, charitable gifts, and income from the sale of its educational products. This support is vital to National Geographic's mission to increase global understanding and promote conservation of our planet through exploration, research, and education.

For more information, please call 1-800-NGS LINE (647-5463) or write to the following address:

National Geographic Society
1145 17th Street N.W.
Washington, D.C. 20036-4688
U.S.A.

Visit the Society's Web site at:
www.nationalgeographic.com.

Composition for this book by the National Geographic Society Book Division. Printed and bound by R.R. Donnelley & Sons, Willard, Ohio. Color separations by Quad Imaging, Washington, D.C. Dust jacket printed by Miken Companies, Inc., Cheektowaga, New York.